# BRANDING BUD

# BRANDING BUD

## THE COMMERCIALIZATION OF CANNABIS

DAVID A. PALESCHUCK

QUICK
AMERICAN
PUBLISHING

PIEDMONT, CA

BRANDING BUD: THE COMMERCIALIZATION OF CANNABIS
Copyright © 2021 David Paleschuck

Published by Quick American Publishing
A division of Quick Trading Co.
Piedmont, California

Printed in the USA
First Printing

ISBN: 9781936807512
eISBN: 9781936807529

Cover Design Concept: David Paleschuck
Cover Design Artwork: Billi Kid
Book Design: Kory Kirby
Production: Christy Quinto
Chief Editor: Andrea Larson

Photographic imagery courtesy as noted

Library of Congress Control Number: 2021930834

*To Benjamin: My love; my joy; my pride.*
*To Stephanie: For giving me the best gift ever.*
*To Toby: Always loved. Never forgotten.*
*To Moe: I really appreciate it.*

# CONTENTS

# AN INNOVATOR'S PERSPECTIVE ON CANNABIS

*by Brian Wansolich, Co-Founder, Leafly.com & Headset.io*

Reading an early manuscript of *Branding Bud: The Commercialization of Cannabis* instantly made me nostalgic for the heady days of 2010, when my partners and I were hard at work launching leafly.com—arguably the largest cannabis website in the world.

As part of that, I learned about building a cannabis brand the hard way, which is to say completely on my own and in a vacuum. And perhaps because of this book, you won't have to endure those same hardships. Written to inform and educate, the perspective *Branding Bud* provides is hugely valuable for entrepreneurs, marketers, and anyone else looking to create a brand presence in the rapidly expanding cannabis industry. Even for legacy players, the insights contained within the book can serve as a new roadmap to help revitalize their brands as they forge ahead in the increasingly competitive cannabis landscape.

David and I first met at an early Marijuana Business Conference in Kissimmee, Florida. The event took place at the Gaylord Palms Resort & Convention Center. Given the fact that Florida had harsh penalties for possession and at the time hadn't yet legalized medical marijuana, this seemed an odd state and venue to host the largest cannabis business conference in the world. Having an ounce of weed in Florida was a felony offense and could land you in jail for five years. But here we were, amongst the guns and gators talking about the newly forming cannabis industry.

The conference went ahead and thankfully brought me into contact with David. At the time, he was Dope Magazine's Vice President of Licensing & Brand Partnerships. I wasn't quite sure what that meant, but I could tell by our initial conversation he came from a place of real-world knowledge and expertise. We talked quite a bit about the rapid evolution in the cannabis industry over the past few years, and the astounding explosion of new product segments and brands that have come along with it. David's grasp of the brand landscape was complete, speaking knowledgeably about how cannabis brands could and should begin differentiating themselves within that landscape.

There, I learned that before entering the cannabis industry, David had worked at American Express, MasterCard, PepsiCo, and Microsoft in marketing and branding. His work for those behemoth companies was not lost in the opacity that typically comes with working for large organizations. Rather, he worked on some extremely visible and effective marketing programs that continue to leave a lasting impression with well-known campaigns like MasterCard's "Priceless" and Pepsi's "Do The Dew." Despite his long working career for world-class brands, David remains humble and eager to soak up all the cannabis industry has to serve. He knows how to push brands to the forefront while orchestrating the behind-the-scene intricacies of brand management and stewardship.

And how, exactly, do you build a standout brand? From my own experience, I see a brand as being a subtle blend between how a company represents itself and how the public perceives that representation. Apart from being a logo and occupying a visual position in the marketplace, a brand is composed of other elements that stretch far beyond the realm of design. This includes a brand's voice—its messaging, content, and social presence. Another part of that blend is customer service and user experience, which directly influence public perception. To have a successful brand, companies must keep these elements in balance.

While branding in the cannabis industry rests on these fundamentals, it is also unique in that the cannabis industry is still evolving. Opportunities like this only come along once in a lifetime, and it behooves us to take advantage of this opportune adventure. Our industry is working through what it wants to be, and as business owners, employees, consumers, and patients, we all play an active role in how that manifests.

While many are here for monetary gain above all else, there are just as many who see cannabis as a panacea, something that can heal the damage of the drug war, provide valuable medicine to patients and generate prosperity in the process. The industry could potentially set itself up in such a way that it incents businesses to build more sustainable models of success, supplanting our current obsession with (unsustainable) monetary growth. This simple plant can do a lot, but to do so, our industry must get its message across, and get it across in a way that engages a broader segment of the population.

*Branding Bud* covers many relevant topics but one that struck me most is the chapter on brand identity and developing cannabis brands. In 2010, when we were developing leafly.com, canna-branding and marketing were firmly rooted in stoner culture. This was fine at the time, as only hardcore cannabis enthusiasts and lovers of weed sought out the stereotypical, counterculture imagery. To be a successful brand at that time, one needed only to cater to this one segment of consumers. Pot leaves, tie-dye, overuse of words like "weed," "420," and "Mary-Jane," not to mention objectifying images of bikini-clad babes. What I found most interesting about this chapter is it looks beyond the typical stoner stereotypes and offers insight into how entrepreneurs can make their brand appealing to the new cannabis customer.

When my co-founding partners and I were creating leafly.com, we realized we had a chance to break the stoner. We saw a once in a lifetime opportunity to give cannabis a more approachable identity and help normalize it in a way that had never been done before. Indeed, the whole point of leafly.com was to make the cannabis buying experience approachable, so we really wanted our branding to reflect that. We were lucky enough to come up with a product that met two needs at once: the need of consumers for clear, understandable information on cannabis products and strains, and the need for dispensaries to get the most accurate, up-to-date menus in front of customers.

Our mission with leafly.com was to demystify cannabis and our product did a lot to make the cannabis experience accessible and pleasant for people who might otherwise have been intimidated by it. The challenge in branding was, of course, making a cannabis-centric product that didn't intimidate people who were already intimidated by cannabis. No easy feat, when you consider how off-putting the decades of stoner stereotypes can be to the average consumer.

How was I to strike a balance between visually representing a cannabis strain database, a trusted, consumer-facing web brand, and cannabis culture simultaneously? This was uncharted territory in terms of brand creation, which made for a serious challenge, albeit a very gratifying one.

For the name, we brainstormed and felt that having at least one minor reference to the plant would be appropriate. The word "Leaf" was neutral enough, while still giving a nod to the fact that our website was about a specific plant.

We also knew that we'd have to communicate our message—"this is about cannabis, but this is for everyone"—at every level. To do this, I went to my trusty color wheel and searched for colors that would be appropriate for the plant—red, green, and purple—without being in your face. Notice that we did not select red, green, or gold, despite the fact that those colors shout "cannabis" loud and clear. We were going for something more sophisticated and subtler.

We did, however, want to use visual design elements that automatically and intuitively conveyed a system of classification, which is what drove us to model our strain tiles after the periodic table. The periodic table of elements is a design that has been drilled into most of our brains since childhood. By setting up our strains in the same layout, we were able to capitalize on that instant familiarity.

Today, our new cannabis data analytics startup, headset.io is bringing really useful information to a different customer: cannabis businesses including retailers, producers, and processors. This time our branding has to be different—perhaps even a little further removed from cannabis—but the concept is the same: create a brand vision and leverage that vision at every customer touchpoint.

Our name "Headset" resonates with both the core smoker as well as the newer, more discrete canna-consumer. "Head" is a common cannabis term. Think "headshops" or "potheads." Set is a nod to the datasets we use to power our product, as well as Timothy Leary's age-old idea of "set and setting." The combined word "headset" evokes awareness and connectivity. We want our customers to understand at an intuitive level, that our service provides them with invaluable information.

Our logo resembles a headset-shaped geometric arc and a color palette that transitions from red to deep purple. Because headset.io is more tangential than perhaps Leafly.com, we moved even further away from the colors of the plant. When our customers see the headset.io logo, we want them to think "information" first, followed closely by "cannabis." Strong brands convey their messages on many levels and the best brands leverage all consumer touchpoints to build a coherent, relevant marketing program.

After years of research and development, I've analyzed, filtered, sliced, and diced large canna-related data sets. The conclusions David has put forth in his book after interviewing hundreds of canna-brand owners, retailers, budtenders, consumers, and patients alike, support the information we see ported through our hesadset.io POS systems. From regional preferences, palates, and form factors to product bundling and basket sales—(among other data points)—I'm pleased to see in-depth qualitative information aligning with the quantitative dataset reflected in headset.io's offering.

Used wisely, *Branding Bud: The Commercialization of Cannabis* can help craft a coherent brand strategy that resonates with cannabis consumers and patients alike. Whether a brand owner, designer, investor, consumer, or simply an interested bystander, *Branding Bud* is a great read for both newbies and industry experts.

Brian Wansolich, Co-Founder, Leafly.com & Headset.io

# OVERVIEW, PURPOSE AND OBJECTIVES

*Branding Bud: The Commercialization of Cannabis* was created with several objectives in mind. While seeking to learn more about a new category of cannabis-infused consumer packaged goods, I was also curious to see how products were packaged (and how that varied across States), as well as what were the inspirations and who are the people behind these new brands.

In seeking to find the answers to the above questions, I was also concerned about product safety and consistency; issues surrounding responsible use and education; and most importantly, assuring our children and society as a whole is protected.

To delve a bit deeper into the book's objectives, I relied on the following pillars:

- Present a critical overview of legal cannabis products and their packaging
- Promote the awareness and responsible use of cannabis
- Support safe, consistent cannabis products, programs and policies
- Raise the industry bar through standards and best practices
- Educate and protect the safety of our children

While seeking to sort through the overwhelming lack of and/or conflicting evidence on cannabis consumption, efficacy, possible dangers, and addictive qualities—my intent was to be fair and objective in presenting the historical and political aspects of cannabis, in order to set the stage for a critical review of the current State legal cannabis products in the U.S. market today.

## PRESENT A CRITICAL OVERVIEW OF LEGAL CANNABIS BRANDS

*Branding Bud* is focused on the branding and packaging aspects of the newly developed legal U.S. cannabis products segment. Designed to review the brands' inspirations, areas of expertise and core competencies, as well as their respective founders' backgrounds, the book seeks to:

- Present a cursory review of the past and present political and historical state of cannabis.
- Briefly touch upon the types of cannabis, their chemical components, and typical efficacy.
- Contextualize cannabis use from the 18th century to its influence on today's pop culture.
- Delineate various cannabis form factors, means of processing, and ways of consuming.
- Cohesively layout the current state of legal U.S. cannabis and cannabis-infused products.
- Create industry standards that bring this segment in line with other CPG industries.

This book will not:

- Discuss the efficacy of cannabis products.
- Compare and contrast any particular products.
- Create a rating system in which any specific products are promoted above others.
- Denigrate or disrespect any products, categories, and/or brand owners.

While the book is focused on branding and packaging—and utilizes materials from the brands describing their products—the book also contains objective information from various testing labs and reports from credible associations, journals, and research firms designed to objectively inform the reader about the products reviewed.

## PROMOTE THE AWARENESS AND RESPONSIBLE USE OF CANNABIS

We hope to eliminate the stigma attached to consuming cannabis, by promoting general awareness, responsible use and public safety education. To that end, there is a list of resources and contacts included at the end of the book.

## SUPPORT SAFE, CONSISTENT CANNABIS PRODUCTS, PROGRAMS AND POLICIES

While public opinion is changing, as denoted throughout this book, there is concern from lawmakers and consumers alike on the dosing and consistency of the cannabis products currently in the market. The Journal of American Medicine (JAMA), published an article in June 2015 titled, "Cannabinoid Dose and Label Accuracy in Edible Medical Cannabis Products", and summarized that "Edible products from three major metropolitan cities including Seattle, San Francisco and Los Angeles—(oddly, Denver was not included)—though unregulated, failed to meet basic label accuracy standards for pharmaceuticals."[1]

Such products may not produce the desired efficacy and/or relief required. Other products contained significantly more THC than labeled, placing consumers at risk of experiencing adverse effects. Because medical cannabis is recommended for specific health conditions, regulation, consistency, and quality assurance are required. As medical and recreational markets continue to grow, it will take large amounts of outside scrutiny and self-regulation of cannabis products and their labeling, packaging, dosing, and consistency. This will be critical to the growing acceptability among lawmakers and consumers alike.

## RAISE THE INDUSTRY BAR THROUGH STANDARDS AND BEST PRACTICES

Typical business practices suggest looking for deep expertise in one's own industry to solve a problem. As business models transform and evolve, organizations can learn from other industries and businesses regardless of the business they are in. Cannabis entrepreneurs should not recreate the wheel. Rather, they should look outward toward other industries to select the best practices and standards to ensure quality and consistency.

## EDUCATE AND PROTECT THE SAFETY OF OUR CHILDREN

Every parent should have a conversation with their children about what cannabis is and what it isn't. Children need to know that unless they are medical cannabis patients, they must not use cannabis. If you have older children at home, they need to know they can get in legal trouble for possessing, selling, or giving away cannabis.

The Federal Government's 2013 Cole Memorandum[2] listed, "Preventing the distribution of cannabis to minors,", as one of its enforcement priorities in allowing state cannabis programs. Locally, many zoning laws requiring medical cannabis dispensaries and recreational stores to be a specific distance away from schools, parks, and child-care centers.

Smoking cannabis near children exposes them to secondhand smoke and its physical and mental effects. Consuming cannabis-infused edibles also has its risks. No matter where or in what form the cannabis is consumed, a parent must never become unable to provide the required care for and proper supervision of their children. A State may consider a parent's incapacitation from cannabis to be a danger to children in the home and could take measures against the parent.

Parents who use cannabis should store any cannabis or cannabis-infused edibles under lock and key away from minors. Many edible cannabis products will appeal to children, and if you allow edibles to be easily obtained by children, you might have your parenting skills and ability questioned by authorities.

It is with this focus that this book was created. I hope you take away insight, value, and context to be utilized personally and/or shared with others you know. If there's one certain thing, you either are or know a cannabis consumer. Now it's time to educate on awareness, acceptance, and responsibility.

David Paleschuck, MBA, CLS, Author, Founder, PALESCHUCK

CHAPTER ONE

# FROM DIME BAGS TO DOSED PORTIONS

Long gone are the days of illegally purchasing "nickel and dime" bags of "weed" on the street corner. In fact, today in at least 28 states, a legally licensed patient can purchase medicinal cannabis or a consumer over the age of 21 can purchase cannabis and cannabis-infused products legally at many recreational stores in states such as Colorado, Washington, Oregon; and voters in Washington, D.C., who approved an initiative to allow recreational use.

For some, it's a way to relax or relieve pain; for others, it's a dangerous and addictive drug. Whatever your thoughts on cannabis, it's hard to deny the impact it has had on American culture and history. In this book, I'll take a brief look at the politics and laws that played a role in shaping marijuana's image in the minds of Americans. I'll seek to inform in a simple, clear manner how people consume cannabis, which companies currently create products and brands that may likely become trusted household names in the future.

By way of example, a new Harris Poll[1] finds that the growing acceptability of cannabis among state lawmakers reflects attitudinal shifts among U.S. residents in the last few years. Support for the legalization of cannabis for both medical treatment and recreational use has increased by 7% in the past four years. The results come from 2,221 U.S. adults surveyed online between February 11th and 17th, 2015.

According to the poll, four in five adults (81%) favor legalizing cannabis for medical use, up from 2011, when three-quarters of Americans indicated the same. Meanwhile, according to Harris, half of Americans are supportive of legalizing cannabis for recreational use (49%), up from 42% who felt that way in 2011. Nearly nine in ten Democrats and independents are in favor of legalizing cannabis for medical treatment (87% and 86%, respectively) and more than half support recreational use (58% and 55%).[2]

About 70% of Republicans support the medicinal use of cannabis, while 23% oppose it. In contrast, 65% of Republicans oppose legalizing the recreational use of cannabis. Only 27% of the Republicans polled support legalizing recreational cannabis.[3]

---

*"About four in five adults say they favor legalizing cannabis for medical use, up from 75% support in 2011"*

*- THE HARRIS POLL (2015)*

---

Cannabis remains illegal on the federal level, but the continuing reform of state marijuana laws is eroding the plant's outlaw status. According to a Gallup Poll,[4] 51% of Americans favor legalization.

Among Colorado voters, a Quinnipiac University Poll[5] found most, "Believe it was a good move to legalize recreational marijuana, but few admit to joining the ranks of new 'imbibers.'" With noticeable gender and age gaps, Colorado voters support legalized recreational marijuana 58% to 38% (males more than females and younger rather than older respondents being more in favor).

Since cannabis still cannot cross state lines—even between states that have both legalized it. Companies are generally, local by nature, for now. All products must be made in state, from seed to sale, so the idea of a multi-state business is first becoming viable. Dixie Elixirs and Mary's Medicinals two of the most successful cannabis companies in Colorado offer multiple products in different formats and have become a few of the first companies to cross state lines by licensing their brands, formulas, and recipes. This allows them to maintain product consistency and expand their market share, both of which are key for any national brand.

Celebrities and well-heeled investors alike have begun seeking new cannabis-related opportunities. The SEC recently allowed California-based grow equipment company Terra Tech Corp. who operates a grow and a dispensary, to register with the Exchange. The SEC made another step in December when they decided they would not enforce federal laws pertaining to investing in canna-businesses. PayPal co-founder, Peter Thiel, jumped on board with a $75 million investment to the Seattle-based Privateer Holdings, who owns Leafly, a cannabis-focused app and the recently launched line of cannabis products by Marley Natural.

> *"If I were to exemplify one trend in the cannabis market that surpasses all other trends, whether it be, the newest infused food, or delivery system, concentrates or topicals. It would simply be cannabis's acceptance. This is a movement we cannot allow to diminish, rather we must continue the push for more freedoms, more studies, more education, and more access to those that need it most."*
> — Dave Inman, Radio Host, State Of Cannabis

Many other celebrities are seeking to cash in on the canna-business. Melissa Etheridge makes a cannabis-infused wine; B-Real of Cypress Hill owns a dispensary; Snoop Dogg has his own vape pen, and Tommy Chong licenses his name and likeness out to many cannabis ventures. The exposure and instant name recognition that these products are receiving because of the face they are attached to is no doubt good for business—but is that enough?

In recent months, TV comedy and drama series have included references to cannabis more often since medicinal and recreational use became legal in many states. Sure, depictions proliferate on cable: "Weeds" was a daring first on Showtime; more recently the working women on Showtime's "Episodes" share a joint in an upscale Hollywood kitchen; the babes on Comedy Central's "Broad City" smoke in the street. The web series "High Maintenance" centers on a pot dealer known only as "The Guy." "Weed" and "weed culture" are prevalent in America's popular culture, albeit just under the surface.

Courtesy: HBO

Courtesy: Comedy Central

Courtesy: VICE Video

Brand marketing and new product development play major roles in the creation of new products and their launch into the market. Most of today's larger players in the industry started growing in their basements or opening medical cannabis dispensaries years ago. Of course, with a market as promising as the cannabis industry there will be lots of money exchanged and invested, and many will become wealthier from it. However, a strong majority of the successful business owners started as grassroots cooperatives and helped to bring cannabis out of the closet and into the mainstream with smart policy reform and advocacy.

Only recently have big names started to attach themselves to a once-taboo product, as there is now little risk of federal prosecution. Without years of hands-on experience managing the plant directly, it seems hard to believe that new growers and investors could be successful, but then again, a consortium of growers, rappers, and/or Rasta legends with world-class investment would have to succeed, right?

One thing is for sure: with the popularity of cannabis and the many new ways to consume it, there will never be a monopoly on any one aspect of legal cannabis. No single brand could ever control the whole market, leaving much room for healthy competition.

*"Nothing is set in stone, and with so many people dreaming of being the Steve Jobs of cannabis, it will be exciting to see what brands can set themselves apart as consistent, high quality and trusted in the years to come."*

- DAVID TRAN, CO-FOUNDER, DOPE MAGAZINE, FAIRCHILD EVENTS

By any reasonable definition, marijuana has "currently accepted medical use in treatment in the United States." Eight states have officially legalized its medical use. The widespread and growing popularity of medical marijuana and its potential for treating a wide range of conditions indicate a growing role in American medicine. These facts refute marijuana's current Schedule I misclassification as a drug lacking "currently accepted medical use"[6] (Gieringer 2002).

A considerable number of organizations representing healthcare professionals, the medical community, and the general public support granting greater access to medical cannabis for patients in need and recognizing explicitly marijuana's medical use both in the United States and in the international community.

While public perception has been a major motivator in this shift, Americans believe marijuana should be legal. Between the need for additional revenue at the state level to help reduce or close budget gaps, and providing solutions to people with serious medical conditions, marijuana's momentum is undeniable.

I'd be remiss, though, if I didn't also state that many questions remain, such as whether or not the government will change its stance on cannabis as a Schedule I drug, and if cannabis's benefits outweigh its risks. The last question is particularly hard to answer as we have very limited long-term data, and what we do have was primarily focused on the risks of cannabis rather than the benefits.

Courtesy: Yahoo Finance

The DEA may move to reschedule cannabis to a lesser schedule, keeping it within the purview of the Controlled Substances Act (CSA) means that it would still be illegal, even for medical use in the absence of FDA approval. Even with FDA approval, a years-long process, it would still require a prescription to obtain, which would do nothing to address legal adult cannabis sales, production, or possession in the states. Removing it from the CSA, or de-scheduling, is what consumers and the industry are calling for, but that is the unlikeliest outcome, even though that's how the US deals with the two most commonly used recreational drugs, alcohol, and tobacco.

## CHAPTER TWO

# A CANNABIS PRIMER

## THC IS THE PRIMARY PSYCHOTROPIC INGREDIENT

That said, THC (tetrahydrocannabinol) also has a wide range of medical benefits and is commonly reported to relieve pain, nausea, and depression, among many other things. Yet its status as an illegal drug has made information about this cannabis compound hard to come by. Here are a few facts worth noting about THC:

### THC Was Discovered In 1964

THC was first isolated and synthesized from the cannabis plant by a scientist in Israel named Dr. Raphael Mechoulam. As a postdoctoral student in the early 1960s, Dr. Mechoulam noticed that the active compounds in morphine and cocaine had been isolated, but no one had isolated the active ingredient in cannabis. The scientist was the first to isolate THC in 1964, marking the start of a long career dedicated to cannabis research.

### THC Is One Of More Than 60 Active Ingredients In Cannabis

Despite being the most recognized ingredient in cannabis, THC is just one of many compounds in the plant with known medical uses. THC belongs to a unique class of compounds called cannabinoids. Since Dr. Mechoulam's discovery, more than 60 other cannabinoids in cannabis have been identified. THC and CBD are the two cannabinoids usually found in the highest concentrations.

### THC Can Protect Brain Cells And Stimulate Their Growth

Contrary to popular belief, THC has been proven to have several positive effects on brain cells. Whereas alcohol and other drugs are neurotoxic, THC is considered a "neuroprotectant," meaning it can protect brain cells from damage caused by things like inflammation and oxidative stress.

What's more, scientists have even shown that THC can promote the growth of new brain cells through a process known as neurogenesis. This effect was first discovered in 2005 by researchers at the University of Saskatchewan. The study's lead author, Dr. Xia Zhang, noted in an interview with Science Daily: "Most 'drugs of abuse suppress neurogenesis. Only cannabis promotes neurogenesis.'"[1]

### Chemicals Like THC Are Found In The Body

Following the discovery of THC, scientists searched for decades for similar chemicals in humans that might explain its effects. In 1992, Dr. Mechoulam and his team made another breakthrough when they discovered a molecule called anandamide.[2]

As it turns out, anandamide is one of a few cannabinoids produced in various parts of the body, including the brain. Similar to the way opioids work by mimicking their natural counterparts (endorphins), chemicals in cannabis mimic naturally occurring cannabinoids called endocannabinoids. Both anandamide and THC act on pathways in the body called cannabinoid receptors. In the brain, anandamide works to regulate mood, sleep, memory, and appetite.

## CANNABIS STRAINS: INDICA VS. SATIVA

Two main "classification" types make up the majority of all cannabis "strains." These two main classifications are popularly known as Cannabis Sativa and Cannabis Indica.

### Cannabis Sativa

*Cannabis Sativa* grows taller and thinner than Indica strains. Sativa strains originated in the equatorial countries of Columbia, Mexico, Thailand, and South East Asia, and thrive in warmer weather. The leaves of a Sativa are narrower than those of an Indica and are typically a lighter shade of green.

Sativa plants have been known to stretch to extraordinary heights of up to 20 feet when grown outside and have much longer vegetation periods.

Once the plant begins to flower, it can take anywhere from 10-16 weeks to fully mature. Since vegetation periods are so long, these plants typically produce a much higher yield than Indica strains (3 oz. to 1 lb. per plant) but possess a lower THC percentage than Indica on average (around 12-16%).

Sativa plants are known to be extremely pungent smelling, with aromas ranging from sweet and fruity, to earthy with undertones of diesel fuel. Many of our favorite Sativa strains such as Cherry AK, Green Crack, Trainwreck, Jack Herer, and J-1 all have a similar sweet and peppery smell that is classic of Sativa. Some strains like Trainwreck will be more peppery, while Cherry AK is extremely sweet-smelling. Although these strains will all provide similar effects, the distinction lies in these differences in smell, formally known as their "terpene profile." Once you are familiar with all the different terpenes that are present in cannabis, it is fairly easy to detect what strain you are smoking based on scent alone.

> "Cannabis Sativa is particularly effective in treating mental and behavioral issues such as stress, anxiety, depression, and ADHD."
>
> - JEFFREY RABER, PH.D., THE WERC SHOP

Sativa strains are known to produce an uplifting and cerebral high that is typically very energizing and stimulating. They are known to make you laugh uncontrollably or engage in in-depth conversations about the meaning of life. These strains typically cause you to analyze the human experience and think creatively, which makes Cannabis Sativa very popular among philosophers, artists, and musicians. Some Sativa has even been found to enhance lights and sounds; making music, movies, and the rest of your surroundings more vibrant than ever before.

Patients looking for the perfect morning medication or daytime relief could benefit from accompanying their breakfast or lunch with a vaporizer packed with Strawberry Diesel or Cherry AK. Both of these strains are known to give you a long-lasting, clear-headed (sometimes cerebral) high that will leave you uplifted and energetic.

## Cannabis Indica

On the contrary, Cannabis Indica is short and stout in composure (2-4 feet tall), and typically yields smaller (1.5 to 2.5 oz. per plant) but higher quality crops (~18% THC) than Cannabis Sativa. The plants are believed to have originated in the Middle East (Pakistan and Afghanistan) and thrive in cooler environments. Indica strains are typically darker green than Sativa and have shorter, fatter leaves.

Since the plants grow so short, they are ideal for indoor growing. The buds are thick and dense, flowering in anywhere from 8-12 weeks. The flavors and smells of Cannabis Indica include; pine, pungent skunk, earth, hash, or a sweet and sugary fruit flavor.

---

*"Most consumers use Cannabis Indica after a long day at work to relieve stress, provide full-body pain relief and help them fall asleep at night."*
- BRAD DOUGLASS, PH.D., THE WERC SHOP

---

The effects produced by Indica strains are very relaxing and narcotic-like, typically providing a full-body, or "couch-lock" effect. Indica is perfect for those days spent curled up on the couch watching TV or surfing the web. However, most people seek Indica after a long day at work to relieve stress, provide full-body pain relief and help them fall asleep at night.

Indica strains are ideal for chronic pain, muscle spasms, anxiety, nausea, appetite stimulation, and sleep deprivation. Individuals who suffer from diseases like multiple sclerosis, fibromyalgia, lupus, sleep apnea, and insomnia tend to benefit from the effects of Cannabis Indica. Patients looking for the ideal Indica to put you straight to sleep should consider trying any strain with OG or Kush in its genetics; our favorite night-time strains include GDP, Pure Kush, and God's Gift. All of which provide significant pain relief coupled with heavy sedative effects.

Cannabis is a complex plant with endless possible strain combinations that are difficult to classify. Categorizing cannabis is far more complex than simply classifying strains as Sativa or Indica. Nevertheless, it is our hope this book will provide basic insight and clarity on the topic, allowing consumers and those with interest to recognize the differences in strains as they might recognize a red or white grape.

---

*"CBD (cannabidiol) has quickly changed the debate surrounding the use of cannabis as a medicine."*
- AH WARNER, CANNABIS BASICS, FOUNDER

---

One of the most common uses of cannabis is as a sleep aid. THC is believed to be responsible for most of cannabis's sleep-inducing effects. On the other hand, studies suggest CBD acts to promote wakefulness, making CBD a poor choice as sleep medicine. The opposite effects of CBD and THC on sleep may explain why some strains of cannabis cause users to feel drowsy while others are known to boost energy.

## CBD: A KEY INGREDIENT IN CANNABIS

While doctors note certain side effects of THC, CBD doesn't affect consumers in the same way. Instead, evidence of CBD's medical benefits continues to grow. Here are a few facts worth noting about this unique compound:

### CBD Is One Of Over 60 Compounds

Found in a class of molecules called cannabinoids, CBD is usually present in the highest concentrations and is, therefore, the most recognized and studied. CBD levels tend to vary among different plant strains. Typically, cannabis grown for recreational purposes often contains more THC than CBD.

However, by using selective breeding techniques, growers have managed to create varieties with high levels of CBD and almost zero levels of THC. These strains are rare but have become more popular in recent years for those seeking specific therapeutic effects.

### CBD Is Non-Psychoactive

Unlike THC, CBD does not cause a high or euphoric effect. CBD is non-psychoactive because it does not act on the same pathways as THC. These pathways, called CB1 receptors, are highly concentrated in the brain and are responsible for the mind-altering effects of THC.

A 2011 review published in Current Drug Safety[7] concludes that CBD "does not interfere with several psychomotor and psychological functions." The authors add that several studies suggest that CBD is "well tolerated and safe" even at high doses.

### CBD Has A Wide Range Of Medical Benefits

Although CBD and THC act on different pathways of the body, they seem to have many of the same medical benefits. According to a 2013 review published in the British Journal of Clinical Pharmacology,[8] studies have found CBD to possess the following medical properties:

## Medical Properties Of CBD Effects

| Medical Properties of CBD | Effects |
|---|---|
| Antiemetic | Reduces Nausea And Vomiting |
| Anticonvulsant | Suppresses Seizure Activity |
| Antipsychotic | Combats Psychosis Disorders |
| Anti-Inflammatory | Combats Inflammatory Disorders |
| Anti-Oxidant | Combats Neurodegenerative Disorders |
| Anti-Tumoral/Anti-Cancer | Combats Tumor And Cancer Cells |
| Anxiolytic/Anti-Depressant | Combats Anxiety & Depression Disorders |

## CBD Reduces The Negative Effects Of THC

CBD seems to offer natural protection against the cannabis high. Numerous studies suggest that CBD acts to reduce the intoxicating effects of THC, such as memory impairment and paranoia. Furthermore, CBD also appears to counteract the sleep-inducing effects of THC, which may explain why some strains of cannabis are known to increase alertness. Both CBD and THC have been found to present no risk of lethal overdose, however, to reduce potential side effects, medical users may be better off using cannabis with higher levels of CBD.

## The FDA And CBD

The FDA considers CBD an "unapproved new drug"—continuing-"many companies are misbranding the products and issuing false claims to consumers. Often these products don't list their ingredients on the product label.", reads the FDA's statement. What's worse, is that the FDA conducted tests on many CBD products and found that in most cases, the products contained very little cannabidiol—if any at all.

---

*"Many companies are misbranding the products and issuing false claims to consumers. Often these products do not even list their ingredients on the product label"*
                                              - U.S. FOOD AND DRUG ADMINISTRATION

---

Accordingly, in late February 2016, the FDA issued a warning letter to companies that manufacture and market hemp oils claiming to be, "Rich In CBD." By promising cures for conditions such as cancer, autism, and epilepsy—none of which have been tested by the FDA—they appear to be violating food and drug labeling laws.

While CBD seems to have therapeutic properties in cell and animal studies, there have been no FDA approved, double-blind, placebo-controlled trials of CBD for humans—which is the only avenue to drug certification and legal medical claims.

A work-around for companies selling CBD is to simply make no medical claims and link to outside independent research, then let buyers draw their own conclusions. While the FDA is focusing on medical claims by CBD makers, many experts remain concerned about a bigger issue: Where exactly is this hemp CBD coming from and what's actually in it?

## CBD-Only Laws

Laws allowing for the use of CBD, but not whole-plant marijuana, for medical reasons provide a shield for politicians trying to blunt marijuana reform.

After Dr. Sanjay Gupta's CNN special called "Weed"[3] in 2014, the U.S. saw a new restrictive type of medical cannabis law pass in Utah—one that only legalized cannabidiol (CBD) and only in the form of oil. Soon after, Alabama, Kentucky, and Wisconsin all passed versions of the bill. There is now a total of 14 states that have legalized CBD-rich oil but no other forms of cannabis use. New York passed a restrictive cannabis law that allows more than just CBD, but smoking is still illegal. New York is one of the 23 states, plus D.C., to have legalized whole-plant medical cannabis. That said, while NY law is very restrictive with a pro-CBD bias, it does allow access to more than just CBD medicine.

With numerous states and D.C. passing whole-plant medical cannabis programs and many others having CBD-only laws, nearly three-quarters of America has medical cannabis laws on the books in some form. Thanks to this massive surge in medical cannabis programs, Congress and presidential candidates are finally beginning to view cannabis legalization as a voting issue. Senator Rand Paul [Rep. Kentucky] was the first to openly court the cannabis industry for donations,[4] and has won many friends within the industry for his political perspective.

Now, conservative politicians in conservative states can support medical marijuana, but with the caveat that it is CBD-only and free of any psychoactive THC. Regrettably, this is also without the numerous medicinal benefits of THC and other cannabinoids, such as lowering ocular pressure in people with glaucoma, helping trigger apoptosis and appetite in cancer patients, helping combat PTSD, anxiety, and more.

## A Sobering Summary

The cannabis plant, and everything in it, is illegal under federal law. And even in states where it is legal, it is not legal to ship cannabis products from state to state or to leave the state with such a product.

With Congress actively debating cannabis legalization, our elected representatives must understand the importance of whole-plant medicine and why single molecule CBD-only laws are not the right approach. Current legislation contains an inherent pro-CBD bias and would completely remove CBD from the Controlled Substances Act while leaving whole-plant cannabis in Schedule II, and Marinol (synthetic THC) in Schedule III.

Even with its anti-THC bias, legislation should be passed to allow for better access to cannabis for research purposes, paving the way for scientific study and data that will allow for, and bring clarity and balance to the discussion.

## TERPENES: WHAT THEY ARE AND WHAT THEY DO

Terpenes are a class of organic hydrocarbons produced by a wide variety of plants and are referred to as terpenoids when denatured by oxidation (drying and curing the flowers). They are the main building block of any plant resin or "essential oil" and contribute to scent, flavor, and color. Many are known to have additional medicinal value. Similar to other plants, terpenes are the main class of *aromatic* compounds found in cannabis and have been proven to interact synergistically with other cannabinoids to provide a range of different effects.

When thinking of "aromatic herbs," one conjures the scents of basil, mint, oregano, rosemary, and sage because of their desired aroma and flavor (or terpene profile) in the kitchen. Cannabis is no different. Terpenes are responsible for the aromas and flavors of cannabis. While over 200 terpenes have been reported in the plant, only a small number have actually been studied for their pharmacological effects.

A study conducted in 1997 by the Swiss Federal Research Station for Agroecology and Agriculture entitled "Essential Oil Of Cannabis Sativa L. Strains"[5] characterized 16 terpenoid compounds in the essential oil of different cannabis strains. The most abundant of which was myrcene. Other terpenes that were present in higher concentrations included alpha-pinene, limonene, trans-caryophyllene, and caryophyllene oxide.

Many terpenes are known to have their own pharmacological value. Alpha-pinene is an organic compound found in the oils of rosemary and sage as well as many species of pine trees. Pinene can increase mental focus and energy, as well as act as an expectorant, bronchodilator, and a topical antiseptic and has been used for thousands of years in traditional medicine to retain and restore memory.

---

*"Because of Limonene's potent anti-carcinogenic and anti-fungal properties, it is thought to be the component protecting cannabis smokers from aspergillus fungi and carcinogens found in cannabis smoke."*

- JEFFREY RABER, PH.D.; THE WERC SHOP

---

Other terpenes such as limonene have relaxing effects and are found in anything with a citrus smell such as oranges, lemons, rosemary, and juniper. Limonene is known to have anti-bacterial, anti-depressant, and anti-carcinogenic properties as well. It is thought to quickly penetrate cell membranes causing other terpenes to be absorbed more rapidly and effectively. Because of Limonene's potent anti-carcinogenic and anti-fungal properties, it is thought to be the component protecting marijuana smokers from aspergillus fungi and carcinogens found in cannabis smoke.

Myrcene is another abundant terpene in cannabis—mainly Sativa— and is a building block for menthol, citronella, and geraniol. This terpene possesses muscle-relaxing, anti-depressant, anti-inflammatory, and analgesic effects among other benefits. Myrcene also affects the permeability of cell membranes, which allows for the absorption of more cannabinoids by brain cells.

## THE ENTOURAGE EFFECT: CHEMICAL TEAMWORK

First described in 1998 by Israeli scientists Shimon Ben-Shabat and Raphael Mechoulam, the basic idea of The Entourage Effect is that cannabinoids within the cannabis plant work together and affect the body in a similar way to the body's own endocannabinoid system.

This theory serves as the foundation for a relatively controversial idea within the pharmacology community that in certain cases, whole plant extractions serve as better therapeutic agents than individual cannabinoid extractions. The Entourage Effect Theory has been expanded by Wagner & Ulrich-Merzenich, who define the benefits of basic whole plant extract synergy as follows:

### Affecting Multiple Areas

Many studies have demonstrated the effectiveness of cannabis as a therapeutic agent for muscle spasms associated with multiple sclerosis. A study conducted by Wilkinson and colleagues determined that whole plant extracts were more effective than THC alone.

### Improving Absorption

The Entourage Effect can also work to improve the absorption of cannabis extracts. Cannabinoids are chemically polar compounds, which make them at times difficult for the body to absorb in isolation. The absorption of topicals provides a prototypical example of this problem. The skin is made up of two layers, also known as a bilayer, which makes it difficult for very polar molecules like water and cannabinoids to pass through. With the assistance of terpenoids like caryophyllene, absorption of cannabinoids are increased and therapeutic benefits achieved.

### Minimizing Adverse Side Effects

The Entourage Effect allows certain cannabinoids to modulate the negative side effects of other cannabinoids. The most fitting example of this is CBD's ability to modulate the perceived negative effects of THC.

Many consumers have heard about (or experienced) the increased anxiety and paranoia sometimes associated with cannabis consumption. Research has shown that CBD can be effective in minimizing the anxiety associated with THC, lowering consumers' feelings of paranoia.

THC, CBD, and terpenoids don't compete with one another. In fact, they work in tandem alongside other cannabinoids to provide therapeutic relief for a wide variety of ailments. We'll see in Chapter 7 how cannabis strains (Indica and Sativa), THC, CBD, terpenes, and other cannabinoids come into play relative to specific products currently on the market.

THE WERC SHOP PRESENTS

**CULTIVAR PROFILE SPOTLIGHT:**
# JACK HERER & TRAINWRECK

**Characterizing Cannabis By Chemical Fingerprint Not Phenotype**

Cannabis is commonly categorized according to physical characteristics, (e.g. Indica, Sativa, Hybrid). Historically, these phenotypic categories have been mapped to broad physiological effects (e.g. Indica = sedating, Sativa = stimulating, Hybrid = in-the-middle). This turns out to have been misguided. Testing data demonstrates that phenotypes rarely correlate with the chemical fingerprint of an individual strain. As a result, presuming effects from physical attributes is both misleading and confusing. A more enlightening system involves categorization by chemical fingerprint. This makes sense as the experiential effects of cannabis directly correlate with chemical composition.

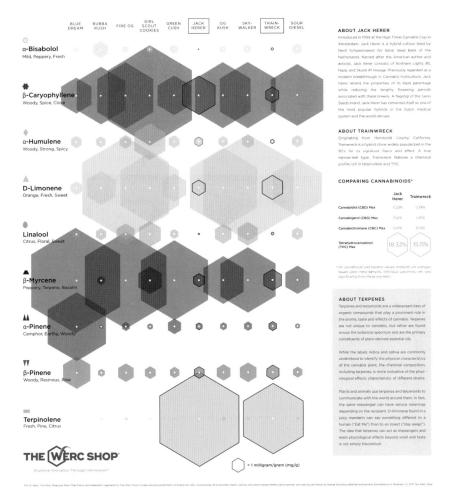

**ABOUT JACK HERER**

Introduced in 1994 at the High Times Cannabis Cup in Amsterdam, Jack Herer is a hybrid cultivar bred by Nevil Schoenmakers for Sensi Seed Bank of the Netherlands. Named after the American author and activist, Jack Herer consists of Northern Lights #5, Haze, and Skunk #1 lineage. Previously regarded as a modern breakthrough in Cannabis horticulture, Jack Herer retains the properties of its Haze parentage while reducing the lengthy flowering periods associated with these breeds. A flagship of the Sensi Seeds brand, Jack Herer has cemented itself as one of the most popular hybrids in the Dutch medical system and the world abroad.

**ABOUT TRAINWRECK**

Originating from Humboldt County, California, Trainwreck is a hybrid clone widely popularized in the 90's for its signature flavor and effect. A true narrow-leaf type, Trainwreck features a chemical profile rich in terpinolene and THC.

**COMPARING CANNABINOIDS***

| | Jack Herer | Trainwreck |
|---|---|---|
| Cannabidiol (CBD) Max | 0.23% | 0.24% |
| Cannabigerol (CBG) Max | 0.61% | 0.51% |
| Cannabichromene (CBC) Max | 0.06% | 0.07% |
| Tetrahydrocannabinol (THC) Max | 18.32% | 15.11% |

*All cannabinoid and terpene values displayed are averages based upon many samples. Individual specimens can vary significantly from these averages.

**ABOUT TERPENES**

Terpenes and terpenoids are a widespread class of organic compounds that play a prominent role in the aroma, taste and effects of cannabis. Terpenes are not unique to cannabis, but rather are found across the botanical spectrum and are the primary constituents of plant-derived essential oils.

While the labels indica and sativa are commonly understood to identify the physical characteristics of the cannabis plant, chemical composition, including terpenes, is more indicative of the physiological effects characteristic of different strains.

Plants and animals use terpenes and terpenoids to communicate with the world around them. In fact, the same messenger can have various meanings depending on the recipient. D-limonene found in a juicy mandarin can say something different to a human ("Eat Me") than to an insect ("stay away"). The idea that terpenes can act as messengers and exert physiological effects beyond smell and taste is not simply theoretical.

**Terpene rows (left labels):**

- α-Bisabolol — Mild, Peppery, Fresh
- β-Caryophyllene — Woody, Spice, Clove
- α-Humulene — Woody, Strong, Spicy
- D-Limonene — Orange, Fresh, Sweet
- Linalool — Citrus, Floral, Sweet
- β-Myrcene — Peppery, Terpene, Balsam
- α-Pinene — Camphor, Earthy, Woody
- β-Pinene — Woody, Resinous, Pine
- Terpinolene — Fresh, Pine, Citrus

**Column headers:** BLUE DREAM, BUBBA KUSH, FIRE OG, GIRL SCOUT COOKIES, GREEN CUSH, JACK HERER, OG KUSH, SKY-WALKER, TRAIN-WRECK, SOUR DIESEL

⬡ = 1 milligram/gram (mg/g)

**THE WERC SHOP**
Enabling Innovation Through Information®

# MARIHUANA

WEED WITH ROOTS IN HELL

NOT RECOMMENDED FOR CHILDREN

CHAPTER THREE

# A BRIEF U.S. CANNABIS HISTORY

## HISTORY AT ODDS

At Jamestown Colony, Virginia in 1619, America's first cannabis law was enacted. However, instead of making the plant illegal, all farmers were mandated to grow "Indian hempseed."

Similar compulsory land cultivation laws were enacted across the colonies into the 1700s. Hemp was considered legal tender in most of the nation from 1631 through the early 1800s. During periods of scarcity, farmers could actually be incarcerated for not producing hemp. For more than 200 years, U.S. citizens could pay their taxes with industrial hemp throughout the country.

Paper money was regularly of little use and value to the colonists, whose economy often revolved around the barter system. The steadfast and universal demand for hemp, along with its uniformity and resistance to deterioration and value compared to other raw produce, made it a standard commodity in the Colony.

In 1776, government officials described hemp as, "A valuable economic commodity to colony and mother country alike," as part of a controlled public awareness campaign.

Neither England nor America were able to cultivate enough hemp to meet their respective needs, and each had to import great quantities from Russia, Hungary, Czechoslovakia, and Poland. In 1809, when John Quincy Adams was serving as the American Consul at St. Petersburg, Russia, he noted seeing "as many as 600 clipper ships flying the American flag, in a two-week period loading principally cannabis hemp bound for England and America, where quality was also in great demand."[1]

According to the 1850s U.S. census, America was then home to no less than 8327 hemp plantations-with the minimum plantation no less than 2000 acres. This equates to at least 16 million recorded acres of hemp cultivated in the U.S.–a number that doesn't even account for the tens of thousands of smaller farms growing, nor the potentially hundreds of thousands of family hemp patches across the nation.

All one needs to do is ponder the municipality names, "Hempstead, NY;" "Hempstead, TX;" Hempfield, PA;" etc. to conclude that industrial hemp was obviously an exceedingly significant part of colony life.

About 90% of all ship sails were made from hemp (the word canvas is actually derived from cannabis). Hemp has always been used for basically all rigging, anchor ropes, nets, shrouds, and uniforms; 80% of all textiles were primarily made with hemp fiber through the 1820s; 75%-90% of the world's paper was made with hemp fiber until 1883, and leftover hemp scraps and clothing were recycled into hemp paper until that time (hence the term "rag" paper); 70-90% of all rope, twine and cordage was made from hemp until 1937, and nearly every city and town in the world had some type of hemp rope making industry.[2]

Until approximately 1800, hemp seed oil was the most used oil for lighting in America and the rest of the planet. It was second only to whale oil between the 1800s and the 1870s. All fine paints and varnishes were made from hemp seed oil and/or linseed oil for thousands of years. According to the National Institute of Oilseed Products, Congressional testimony against the 1937 Marijuana Transfer Tax Law, 58,000 tons of hemp seed were used in American paints and varnishes in 1935 alone. After the Marijuana Tax Act was passed, the hemp oil business was cannibalized by Dupont's petrochemicals.

Surely this story of engineered inequality cannot be told in full without sharing the nefarious role of multi-millionaire Andrew Mellon in cannabis prohibition. Mellon, who served as U.S. Secretary of the Treasury from 1921-1932, was one of America's richest men, paid the third-highest income tax in the country, behind only John Rockefeller and Henry Ford.

He was born into tremendous wealth and became an extraordinarily successful lumber and coal businessman. He later joined, and then took ownership of, his father's banking firm, T. Mellon & Sons. Mellon assisted with the formation of the Union Trust Company and the Union Savings Bank of Pittsburgh, which loaned Dupont nearly 80% of the funds needed to grow its petrochemical enterprises. Melon then expanded his own industrial activities in oil, steel, shipbuilding, and construction. His financial backing also supported enormous conglomerates involved with aluminum, industrial abrasives, and coke. Mellon financed the refinery that grew into the giant Aluminum Company of America (ALCOA).

He'd partnered with Edward Goodrich Acheson in manufacturing the inorganic compound silicon carbide, a revolutionary abrasive, and formed Carborundum Company. He created an entire industry by way of financing Heinrich Koppers, inventor of coke ovens that converted industrial sludge into coal gas, coal tar, and sulfur. Coke is a fuel with very high carbon content. The more commonly used form of coke is man-made, derived from oil refinery coker units or other cracking processes, and is known as petroleum coke or "pet coke."

Mellon's petrochemical and banking wealth peaked at $200-400 million dollars in 1929. And in 1930, just seven years before the abrupt passage of the Marijuana Tax Act, and two years before the end of Mellon's service as Secretary of the Department of the Treasury, he created the Federal Bureau of Narcotics, now known as the Drug Enforcement Administration (DEA).

Further, Secretary Mellon's then nephew-in-law-to-be, Harry Anslinger, was appointed as the first Commissioner to this new Federal Bureau of Narcotics. It was Anslinger who presided over the late-night proceedings that culminated in the 1937 Marijuana Tax Act,

Today's federal drug law making the possession of marijuana a crime has its origins in legislation that was passed in an atmosphere of hysteria during the time. Rooted with prejudices against Mexican immigrants and African Americans associated with marijuana use, this racially weighted history lives on today, driven by past myths and propaganda.

Law enforcement's perspective of marijuana is indelibly shaped by the fact that it was initially connected to immigrants, people of color, and poor communities in this country. By the early 1930s, more than 30 states had prohibited the use of marijuana.

As alcohol Prohibition was coming to an end, the Bureau Of Narcotics Commissioner Harry Anslinger was looking for new ways to keep his Agency in business. He soon became the architect of Prohibition. His case rested on two assertions: 1.) "Marijuana caused insanity;" and 2.) "It pushed people toward horrendous acts of criminality."[3]

Anslinger testified that even a single marijuana cigarette could, "Induce a homicidal mania, prompting people to want to kill those they loved." This narrative had a great effect at Congressional hearings leading to the enactment of the Marijuana Tax Act of 1937.

Cannabis Fluid Extracts, Circa 1933
Photo Credit: Allie Beckett
Courtesy: Oaksterdam University

In 1951, a reputable researcher was called to testify. Dr. Harris Isbell, Director of Research at the Public Health Service Hospital in Lexington, KY, disputed the insanity, crime and addiction theories, telling Congress, "Smoking marijuana has no unpleasant after-effects; no dependence is developed on the drug, and the practice can easily be stopped."

Despite the testimony, Congress ratcheted up penalties creating sentences ranging from 5-99 years, without parole or probation, for sale, possession, or administration of narcotic drugs. The rationale was not that marijuana itself "caused insanity and criminality;" rather it was a "steppingstone" to heroin addiction. The country accepted this punitive approach to sentencing, as long as minorities and the poor paid the price. But, by the late 1960s, "weed" was becoming popular with white college students from the middle and upper classes.

Seeing white lives ruined by marijuana laws altered public attitudes about harsh sentencing, and in 1972, the National Commission on Drug Abuse released a report arguing the approach.

The commission concluded that criminalization was, "Too harsh a tool to apply to personal possession even in the effort to discourage use," and that, "The actual and potential harm of use of the drug is not great enough to justify intrusion by the criminal law into private behavior, a step which our society takes only with the greatest reluctance." Nixon's administration dismissed these ideas.[4]

Since the mid-1970s, virtually all states softened penalties for marijuana possession; and over time we have seen this momentum slowly build. While the federal government has taken great steps away from irrational enforcement, it clings to policies that have origins steeped in racism and prejudice.

The Justice Department's decision not to sue states that legalize marijuana, so long as they have strong enforcement rules, eases the tension between state and federal laws slightly, but still leaves many legal issues unresolved. As we start to better understand the long-term effects (benefits and detriments) of cannabis consumption in all forms of ingestion, we will be better able to regulate its acceptance, popularity, and use within our society. Many people assume that marijuana was made illegal through some kind of process involving scientific, medical, and government hearings; that it was to protect the citizens from what was determined to be a dangerous drug.

Other accounts show a much different picture. Those who voted on the legal fate of this plant never had the facts but were dependent on information supplied by those who had a specific agenda to deceive lawmakers. Some say that the very first federal vote to prohibit marijuana was based entirely on a documented lie on the floor of the Senate.

For most of human history, marijuana has been completely legal. It's not a recently discovered plant, nor has it been regulated by long-standing laws. Marijuana has been illegal for less than 1% of the time that it's been in use. Its known uses go back further than 7,000 B.C., and it was legal as recently as when Ronald Reagan was a boy.

## South Of The Border

In the early 1900s, western states developed significant tensions regarding the influx of Mexican Americans. The Mexican Revolution in 1910 spilled over the border with many immigrants as well. Later in the decade, tensions developed between the small farmer and the large farms that used cheaper Mexican labor.

One of the "differences" seized upon during this time was the fact that many Mexicans smoked marijuana and had brought the plant with them. It was through this, that California passed the first state marijuana law, outlawing "preparations of hemp, marijuana or loco weed."

While one of the first state laws outlawing marijuana may have been influenced by Mexicans using the drug, oddly enough, Mormons were also using it, as they (Mormons) traveled to Mexico as missionaries in 1910 and came back to Salt Lake City with marijuana. It was the Church's reaction that contributed to the state's new marijuana law.

Other states quickly followed suit with marijuana prohibition laws, including Wyoming (1915), Texas (1919), Iowa (1923), Nevada (1923), Oregon (1923), Washington (1923), Arkansas (1923), and Nebraska (1927). These laws tended to be specifically targeted against the Mexican American population.

When Montana outlawed marijuana in 1927, The Butte Montana Standard reported a legislator's comment: "When some beet field peon takes a few traces of this stuff (marijuana), he thinks he has just been elected president of Mexico, so he starts to execute all his political enemies." In Texas, a Senator said on the floor of the Senate: *"All Mexicans are crazy, and this stuff (marijuana) is what makes them crazy."*

A Public Service Announcement From 1935
Courtesy: National Museum Of American History

## Cannabis And The Fringe

As marijuana and jazz traveled from New Orleans to Chicago, and then to Harlem it became an indispensable part of the music scene. It found its way into the language of the "negro" hits of the time including Louis Armstrong's "Muggles," Cab Calloway's "That Funny Reefer Man," and Fats Waller's "Viper's Drag."

And while Mexican immigrants had been pouring into the South and Midwest, New York's Harlem was the scene of a vast influx of Negroes from the West Indies and the Southern United States. By 1930, New York's African American population numbered over 300,000. More African Americans lived in New York than in Birmingham, Memphis and St. Louis combined.

Some of these newcomers eventually became prominent business and civic leaders in the community; most found opportunities as limited as they had been back home. Unable to better their condition, they sought ways of making the intolerable tolerable. Some resorted to music with its "charms to soothe the savage beast." Others resorted to drugs such as heroin and especially marijuana, a drug that was no stranger to the West Indian.

On July 30, 1914, the New York Times had commented that "Devotees of hashish are now hardly numerous enough here to count."[5] By January 11, 1923, it proclaimed that marijuana had become the city's "latest habit-forming drug."[6] Even Scientific American noted an increase in the use of marijuana in the city. By 1932, the Bureau of Narcotics also felt that it was widespread enough in the city to warrant at least passing mention in its Annual Report on "Traffic in Opium and Other Dangerous Drugs for the Year Ended December 1931."

The abuse of the drug is noted among the Latin American or Spanish-speaking population. The sale of cannabis cigarettes occurs to a considerable degree in states along the Mexican border and in cities of the Southwest and West, as well as in New York, and, in fact, wherever there are settlements of Latin Americans.

Most of the marijuana users in the city lived around 110th Street and Fifth Avenue, with some spillover into the Broadway area above 42nd Street. Hundreds of marijuana dens were said to be flourishing in Harlem. Some estimated that there were more "tea pads" than there had been speakeasies at the height of Prohibition.

## FEDERAL APPROACHES TO ALCOHOL AND DRUG PROHIBITION

During this time, the U.S. was also dealing with alcohol Prohibition, which lasted from 1919 to 1933. Alcohol Prohibition was extremely visible and debated at all levels, while drug laws were passed without the general public's knowledge. National alcohol Prohibition happened through the mechanism of an amendment to the constitution. Earlier (1914), the Harrison Act was passed, which provided federal tax penalties for opiates and cocaine.

The federal approach is important. It was considered at the time that the federal government did not have the Constitutional power to outlaw alcohol or drugs. It is because of this that alcohol Prohibition required a Constitutional Amendment.

At that time in our country's history, the judiciary regularly placed the 10th Amendment in the path of congressional regulation of "local" affairs, and direct regulation of medical practice was considered beyond congressional power under the Commerce Clause (since then, both provisions have been weakened so far as to have almost no meaning).

In 1930, a new Division of the Treasury Department was established, The Federal Bureau of Narcotics, and Harry J. Anslinger was named Director. This, if anything, marked the beginning of an all-out war against marijuana.

---

*"The primary reason to outlaw marijuana is its effect on the degenerate races."*
*"Marijuana is an addictive drug which produces in its users, insanity, criminality and death."*
*"Reefer makes darkies think they're as good as white men."[7]*

                                                        - HARRY ANSLINGER

---

Since drugs could not be outlawed at the federal level, the decision was made to use federal taxes as a way around the restriction. In the Harrison Act, legal uses of opiates and cocaine were taxed (supposedly as a revenue need by the federal government, which is the only way it would be sustained in the courts), and those who didn't follow the law found themselves in trouble with the Treasury Department.

Anslinger was an extremely ambitious man, and he recognized the Bureau of Narcotics as an amazing career opportunity—a new government agency with the opportunity to define both the problem and the solution. He immediately realized that opiates and cocaine wouldn't be enough to help build his agency, so he latched onto marijuana and started to work on making it illegal at the federal level.

Anslinger immediately drew upon the themes of racism and violence to draw national attention to the problem he wanted to create. He also promoted and frequently read from "Gore Files"—wild reefer-madness-style tales of ax murderers including marijuana, sex, and African Americans. Some quotes that have been widely attributed to Anslinger include:

*"By the tons, it is coming into this country—the deadly, dreadful poison that racks and tears not only the body but the very heart and soul of every human being who once becomes a slave to it in any of its cruel and devastating forms"* [8]

*"Three-fourths of the crimes of violence in this country today are committed by dope slaves—that is a matter of cold record."* [9]

## WHEN TRUTH BATTLES PERCEPTION

Harry Anslinger got some additional help from William Randolf Hearst, who had lots of reasons to help. Hearst had invested heavily in the timber industry to support his newspaper chain and didn't want to see the development of hemp paper in competition. He had lost approximately 800,000 acres of timberland to Pancho Villa. Lastly, printing stories created by Anslinger and his agency about marijuana causing violence sold newspapers, making him richer. Some samples from the San Francisco Examiner (A Hearst Paper) include:

> Further, Hearst and Anslinger were supported by Dupont and other pharmaceutical companies in an effort to outlaw cannabis. Dupont had patented Nylon* and wanted hemp removed as competition. The pharmaceutical companies could neither identify nor standardize cannabis dosages, and with the prevalence of cannabis, consumers could grow their own medicine and not have to purchase it from commercial companies. Combined, this set the stage For The Marijuana Tax Act of 1937.

## THE MARIJUANA TAX ACT OF 1937 AND BEYOND

1937 Marijuana Tax Stamp
Courtesy: www.kyhempsters.com

After two years of planning, Anslinger brought his plan to Congress complete with a dossier full of sensational Hearst editorials and stories of ax murderers who had smoked marijuana. It was a remarkably short set of hearings. The one fly in Anslinger's ointment was the appearance by Dr. William C. Woodward, the legislative council of the American Medical Association.

Woodward started by slamming Anslinger and the Bureau of Narcotics for distorting earlier AMA statements that had nothing to do with marijuana and making them appear to be AMA endorsements for Anslinger's view.

He also reproached the legislature and the Bureau for using the term marijuana in the legislation and not publicizing it as a bill about cannabis or hemp. At this point, marijuana was a sensationalist word used to refer to Mexicans smoking a drug and had not been connected in most people's minds to the existing cannabis/hemp plant. Thus, many who had legitimate reasons to oppose the bill weren't even aware of it. In the end, the Act passed which changed the face of cannabis in America for years to come.

Time will tell if the 21st Amendment that repealed alcohol Prohibition in the 1930s is similar to that of cannabis Prohibition today. While many see no similarity from an efficacy perspective, they do, however, concede there are similarities from a legal and political perspective.

Craft brewers of the 1930s were stymied by government regulations that restricted open trade; much like what small, legal cannabis growers are facing today. Eventually, the liquor industry was taken over by large conglomerates disliked by many of the day's smaller craft brewers. In the same way that some prefer artisan craft beers, wines, and/or coffee to industrial breweries, vineyards and greenhouses-given time–a similar evolution will most likely shape the cannabis industry.

Cannabis companies of today are experiencing similar "restricted open trade" regulations to those of their alcohol Prohibition predecessors, says Josh Kirby, President of Kinslips™, a maker of cannabis-infused sub-lingual breath strips. "Since our products are illegal on the federal level, but not on some state levels, our expansion strategy is somewhat unique. We focus, first and foremost, on formulating quality, consistent and discrete cannabis products; we then license those formulas, along with our brand to reliable licensees." He continues:

---

*"Despite these discrepancies between state and federal laws, brand and product licensing allows us to have a presence in other markets while minimizing legal risk. It also allows us to leverage local talent and knowledge within each market we serve."*
                                                      - JOSH KIRBY, FOUNDER, KINSLIPS

---

Regardless of whether you see cannabis as a recreational, therapeutic, or medicinal substance—or—none of the above, it's imperative that we maintain and monitor rules and regulations that ensure the safety of consumers and society as a whole.

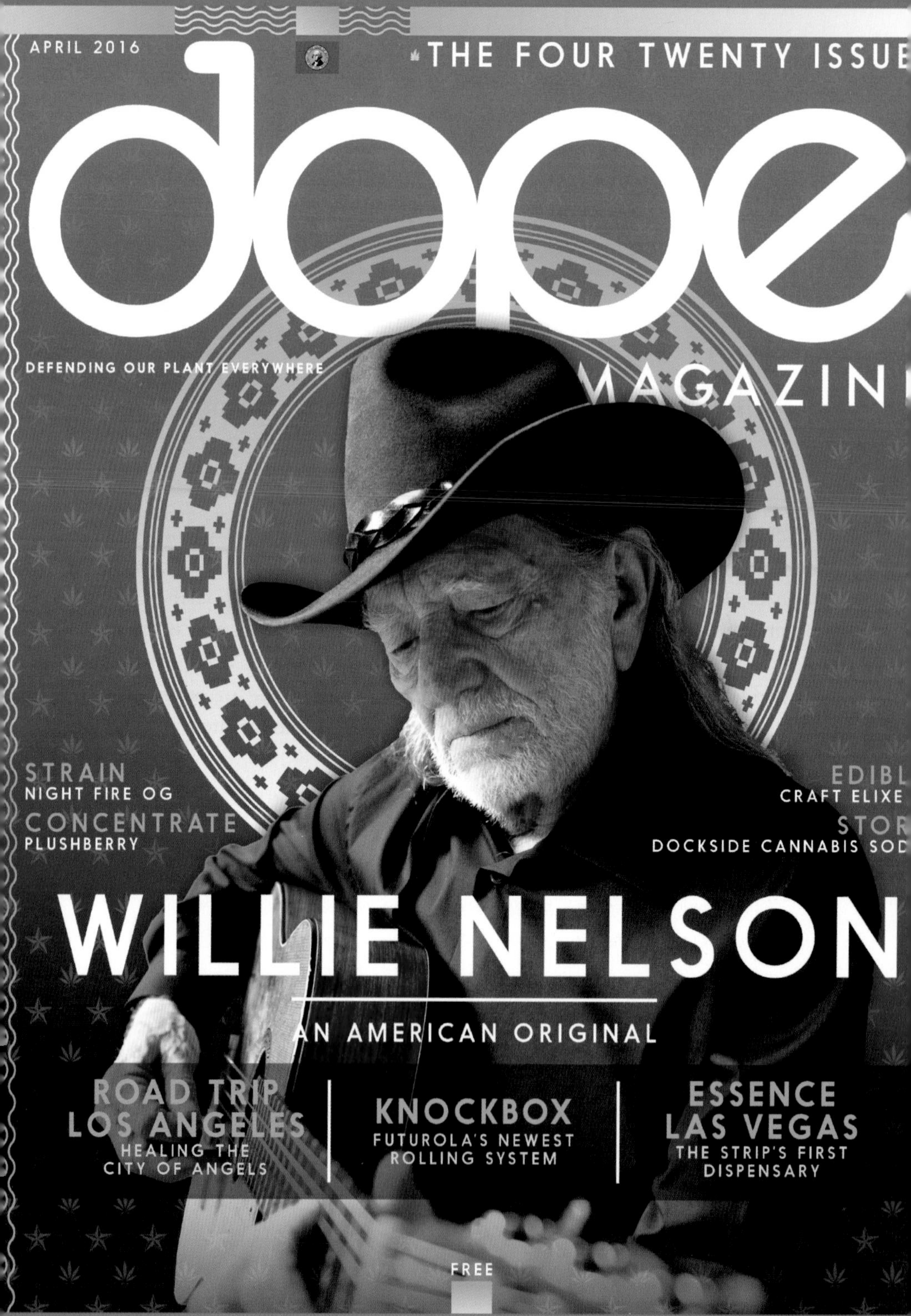

APRIL 2016

THE FOUR TWENTY ISSUE

# dope

## MAGAZINE

DEFENDING OUR PLANT EVERYWHERE

STRAIN
NIGHT FIRE OG
CONCENTRATE
PLUSHBERRY

EDIBLE
CRAFT ELIXE
STOR
DOCKSIDE CANNABIS SOD

# WILLIE NELSON

## AN AMERICAN ORIGINAL

**ROAD TRIP
LOS ANGELES**
HEALING THE
CITY OF ANGELS

**KNOCKBOX**
FUTUROLA'S NEWEST
ROLLING SYSTEM

**ESSENCE
LAS VEGAS**
THE STRIP'S FIRST
DISPENSARY

FREE

CHAPTER FOUR

# THE CREATION OF CANNABIS STEREOTYPES

## CANNABIS IN COUNTERCULTURE AND THE ANTI-ESTABLISHMENT

Since the 1920s, associations between marijuana, counterculture, and fringe lifestyles have mainstream America viewing the substance and its users as subversive and deviant. During Prohibition (1920-1933), men and women gathered in speakeasies (nightclubs that served illegal liquor) to drink, dance, listen to jazz, and smoke. Jazz songs reflected the popularity of marijuana among musicians who often "lit up" and "got high" on hand-rolled "joints" between sets. "Tea Pads" similar to opium dens, where customers could relax and smoke cannabis in relative comfort, were established in cities such as New York and San Francisco.

> *"Smoking pot makes you a criminal and a revolutionary. As soon as you take your first puff, you are an enemy of society."*
> - 1960's COUNTERCULTURE LEADER JERRY RUBIN

Cannabis use was so widespread by the 1930s that moral crusaders, public health reformers, and the Federal Bureau of Narcotics engaged in anti-pot campaigns that characterized marijuana as a threatening substance in PSA's and movies such as *"Reefer Madness"* (1936), which warned that marijuana use could lead to rape, suicide, and manslaughter. Yet, the popularity of cannabis continued to grow during the post-World War II era.

The drug's illegal status only continued to increase its appeal to disaffected youth who reveled in dissident behavior directly challenging mainstream conformity. Allen Ginsberg's highly controversial "Howl and Other Poems" (1956) and Jack Kerouac's "On The Road" (1957) flaunted excessive marijuana use while defining the 1950s Beat culture as well as the hippie movement of the 1960s and 1970s. Cannabis featured prominently in the anti-Vietnam War protests, the Free Speech Movement, counterculture "happenings" and the music of the 1960s.

The euphoria and sense of community experienced by users created a daring culture of unity-in-rebellion. Popular music groups such as The Rolling Stones, The Grateful Dead, The Beatles, and many others flaunted excessive cannabis use both in their lyrics and lifestyles.

Courtesy: Life Magazine      Courtesy: High Times Magazine      Courtesy: Time Magazine      Courtesy: Time Magazine

## FROM PRESIDENTS TO POP CULTURE

As cultural attitudes about cannabis have evolved, the presidential interaction with the substance has too. During the late 18th and early 19th centuries, there was a hashish boom in France. Influenced by French enlightenment philosophy and other French social trends like marijuana use, our founding fathers were certainly influenced - if not, under the influence - of cannabis. By the mid-1800s, more cannabis medicines were being used in Europe and the U.S., as influenced by the pioneering research of doctors such as Dr. W.B. O'Shaughnessy bringing the medicinal use of cannabis back from India. Additionally, the Mexican American War from 1846 to 1848 also spread the popularity of marijuana.

The early 1900s witnessed U.S. law crackdown on substances of all sorts including cannabis. The cultural attitudes behind Prohibition were reflected in presidential interactions, or lack thereof, with cannabis during this era. That is, until the 1960s when adolescents brought it back into the cultural forefront. It makes sense that by today's standards, with so much moving towards the legalization of cannabis, our current president, is the most vocally open about his cannabis use among the presidents in office since its Prohibition.

## Presidential Cannabis Use

George Washington was a known advocate for the growing of hemp as a cash crop. In his writings, Washington referenced the hemp that comes from India, *Cannabis Indica*. His August 7, 1765 diary entry,[1] *"Begin to separate the male from the female (hemp) plants,"* describes a harvesting technique used to enhance the potency for smoking cannabis, among other reasons."

Courtesy: The City Sentinel        Courtesy: The City Sentinel

Contemporaries of Washington, both Thomas Jefferson and Benjamin Franklin were ambassadors to France during this era and may have partaken in the hashish trend while abroad: "Their celebrity status and progressive revolutionary image afforded them ample opportunities to try new experiences."[2] Like Washington, Thomas Jefferson also grew hemp on his farm and while we do not know for sure if he used hemp for smoking, Jefferson's diary contains references to growing the plants in such a way that imply recreational use. It has been reported that Jefferson, "Smuggled Chinese hemp seeds to America."[3]

James Madison and James Monroe were both exposed to smoking hemp during this era. Madison, "Was once heard to say that smoking hemp "Inspired him to found a new nation on democratic principles."[4] James Monroe, like Jefferson and Franklin, was exposed to hashish use when he was the Ambassador to France, and it is reported he continued smoking until his death at the age of 73.

John Quincy Adams, who lived in Russia when he was young, wrote a report in 1810 called, "On The Culture And Preparing Of Hemp In Russia."[5] It is not known whether he smoked any of his crop, though some believe it is likely.

Military men Andrew Jackson, Zachary Taylor, and Franklin Pierce are known to have smoked cannabis with their troops. In one of his personal letters, Pierce, "Wrote to his family that it was about 'the only good thing' about that war."[6] An interesting historical note on the Mexican American War, author Chris Conrad states that during this conflict, "Cannabis was twice as popular among American soldiers in the Mexican War as in Vietnam."[7]

Reflecting the youth counterculture trends of the 1960s, the next president with any known history of cannabis use is John F. Kennedy. A biography[8] notes that while smoking cannabis with friends, Kennedy said, "Suppose the Russians did something now."

Courtesy: The Nation

Courtesy: People Magazine

While it is not known whether president Jimmy Carter smoked cannabis or not, he was perhaps the most progressive President with regards to his attitudes about laws regarding the substance. He supported an Amendment to Federal Law that would, "Eliminate all federal criminal penalties for the possession of up to one (1) ounce of marijuana."[9] Famously, it is alleged that Carter's son smoked cannabis with Willie Nelson on the roof of the White House.

Bill Clinton is famous for saying he "didn't inhale" when he described trying cannabis in his college years at Oxford University. Although, perhaps Clinton was really telling the truth about his cannabis use in that simple statement; his fellow Oxford attendee, the late Christopher Hitchens, noted Mr. Clinton's preference for space brownies rather than smoking.

Courtesy: Time Magazine

George W. Bush is known for having a "wilder" lifestyle during his youth before 1974, admitting to having indulged in cocaine, though his use of cannabis is possible but not confirmed.

Perhaps the most candid of our presidents about his use of cannabis, Barack Obama admitted to smoking cannabis when he was in high school in his 1995 autobiography, "Dreams From My Father."[10] Famously referring to Clinton's remark about cannabis, "When I was a kid, I inhaled, frequently. That was the point."

Courtesy: Ballzbeatz

### "Reefer Madness"

The government-sponsored propaganda film was released in 1936, exaggerating the dangers of the drug to warn parents and children of cannabis use.

### Making It Illegal

The first step to criminalizing cannabis was The 1937 Marijuana Tax Act that put a tax on marijuana. Those who didn't pay the high taxes could be arrested and/or fined. In 1969, the 1937 Act was ruled unconstitutional, leading to marijuana being added to the Controlled Substance Act in 1970, making it illegal.

Courtesy: Etsy

### Woodstock

One of the most famous music and pro-cannabis events in history, the 1969 event in Bethel, NY brought together some 500,000 people for three days of peace, love, music, and marijuana.

### "Easy Rider"

In the 1969 movie, Peter Fonda and Dennis Hopper take a road trip filled with marijuana use, meeting Jack Nicholson along the way. In 2009, Fonda shared that real marijuana had been used in the campfire scene where Nicholson's character smokes pot for the first time.

Courtesy: Christies

Courtesy: DGO

### NORML

Founded in 1970, NORML—the National Organization for the Reform of Marijuana Laws—has helped to decriminalize marijuana for adults and fights for the legalization and taxation of marijuana.

Courtesy: Lowey Institute

### Vietnam War

Daily marijuana consumption among soldiers stationed in Vietnam reached 14%[11], according to a 1971 Department of Defense survey.

Courtesy: Reddit

### Cheech & Chong

The pot-loving comedy duo Cheech and Chong released several marijuana-related movies and comedy albums in the 70s and 80s such as 1978's *"Up In Smoke"* and the 1972 album *"Big Bambu."*

### Drug Enforcement Administration

The DEA was founded in 1973 by President Richard Nixon to combat drug use and distribution in the U.S. and around the world.

Courtesy: Wikipedia

Courtesy: Movies Anywhere

### *"Fast Times At Ridgemont High"*

Actor Sean Penn played stoner and surfer, Jeff Spicoli, in the 1982 comedy, "Fast Times At Ridgemont High" at one point saying: *"All I need are some tasty waves and a cool buzz."*

### *"Dazed And Confused"*

This 1993 movie, starring Matthew McConaughey and Ben Affleck, followed a group of pot-smoking teenagers on their last day of high school in 1976.

Courtesy: Town & Country Magazine

Courtesy: www.impawards.com

### *"Harold And Kumar Go To White Castle"*

In this 2004 comedy, two stoners, played by John Cho and Kal Penn, go on a hunt for White Castle after watching a commercial for the fast-food restaurant while smoking marijuana.

We've come a long way since Bob Dylan's "Rainy Day Woman"—with its chorus, "Everybody must get stoned"—was originally banned in radio stations in 1966. Over the years, depictions of cannabis in entertainment—from Cheech & Chong to the Harold and Kumar movies—have become more mainstream, and in many ways, stereotyped.

The comedy team of Cheech and Chong made films such as "Up In Smoke" that extolled the pleasures of smoking pot at a time the subject was still taboo. "When troubled times begin to bother", "They sang, "I take a toke and all my cares go up in smoke." On the fringes of American society, it was usually possible to find activists who wanted to "legalize it," as the reggae artist Peter Tosh famously sang. Efforts to legalize the substance in the mid-1970s failed.

With 23 states and the District of Columbia having now legalized medical marijuana—Colorado and Washington legalized recreational use—the media has featured lively debate and have run articles supporting this cause. The New York Times editorial page published several high-profile pieces[12] that call for making pot legal at the national level and call out specific steps to be taken to ensure that the industry evolves safely.

Thirty years after Cheech & Chong popularized the myth of "stoners" as amiable goofballs, today's film and television producers are instead portraying pot smokers as regular folks from all walks of life.

Examples supporting this are the Harold and Kumar films center on a stoner investment banker and medical school candidate. In the art-house film, "The Wackness," Sir Ben Kingsley plays a pot-smoking psychiatrist.

On TV, "Weeds," which became a hit on cable network Showtime following its 2005 debut, revolves around a widowed mom who deals dope to make ends meet. Some culture watchers say these new portrayals promote the consumption of illegal drugs among children, while the film and TV producers argue they simply reflect a change in society.

Many say these relatively recent depictions would have been harder to present in the past with U.S. Administrations backing the "War On Drugs," which dates to the early 1970s, including the Reagan White House's "Just Say No" campaign of the 1980s.

---

*"Political climates and cultural climates go together. That was a more conservative era in lots of ways."*

- BRUCE MIRKEN, MARIJUANA POLICY PROJECT

World Health Organization researchers released a study[13] stating Americans lead the world in marijuana use with more than 42% of U.S. citizens acknowledging having tried cannabis. That amounts to just over 125 million Americans.

Hollywood players say their portrayal of marijuana use is not meant to encourage anyone to smoke pot. Rather, they just want to make it part of the storyline to reflect today's society.

This doesn't sit well with the conservative Parents Television Council, which has noticed the growth in marijuana-themed TV shows and movies and worries the portrayals will boost cannabis smoking by children. "If kids can be influenced to smoke cigarettes, which are illegal to sell to minors, why should we believe that a child would not be as inclined to smoke marijuana, which is not legal?" asked, a spokeswoman for the group.

In *"Harold and Kumar Go to White Castle"* and its 2008 sequel, *"Harold and Kumar Escape from Guantanamo Bay"*, the key characters are of Asian and Indian descent. The filmmakers wanted, in part, to, "Break the stereotype that those ethnic groups are too rule-bound," said writer and director Jon Hurwitz.

Even Tommy Chong and Cheech Marin, the top pot comedy team of the 1970s, said marijuana movies these days differ from their brand of pot humor. *"Ours is more primitive. Theirs is more sophisticated"*, Chong said.

How did we reach this tipping point? How have we come to the brink of ending the national Prohibition against a substance that's been condemned for decades as a danger to health and a gateway to harder, more addictive drugs? The following calls out economic, demographic, and generational reasons for the change:

### Generational Change

Baby boomers are now grandparents. This is one of the most important factors driving the national debate. Baby boomers grew up in an era when the use of pot was quite common. Even if a person from the boomer generation did not consume themselves, they knew someone-often friends or family who did.

### The Failed War On Drugs

Often compared to the Prohibition Era, when Congress tried to ban alcohol, it has been clear that the focus on the legality of the sale and use of drugs-rather than on the provision of services to addicts-has resulted in bloated prisons and hugely expensive policing operations;

neither of which has really stemmed the sale of these substances. Indeed, the fact that drugs such as marijuana have been illegal has spurred an unregulated criminal market that preys on disadvantaged Americans who often depend on this as a source of money.

---

*"Penalties against drug use should not be more damaging to an individual than the use of the drug itself. Nowhere is this clearer than in the laws against the possession of marijuana in private for personal use."*

— FORMER PRESIDENT JIMMY CARTER, MESSAGE TO CONGRESS, AUGUST 2, 1977

---

## The Prison-Industrial Complex

The failure of the "War on Drugs" has been part of the reason that we have seen the explosive growth of the prison-industrial complex that incarcerates millions of Americans, including a disproportionate number of African-Americans.

## State Experimentation

Over the past decade, numerous states have legalized the use of marijuana for medical purposes, and most recently, Colorado, Washington, and Oregon for recreational purposes. Each time a state government takes this step, it supports legalization. The states offer models to other states, and perhaps the federal government, as to best practices, business models, and key findings.

## Medical Research

Thus far, there is no medical evidence that the drug has horrendous effects if used in moderation and, just as important, it is much safer both in its effects and after-effects than legal substances such as alcohol. Moreover, there is growing evidence that the drug can be used to help with ailments such as Glaucoma, MS, severe migraines, and other kinds of diseases. To be sure, the verdict is still out, and research must continue, but at this point, there is not sufficient evidence to justify the ban.

---

*"...not because of sound science, but because of its absence, marijuana was classified as a Schedule I substance..."*

— DR. SANJAY GUPTA, CNN[14]

---

## Capitalism

As with almost everything else in the U.S., markets can have a powerful impact on public opinion. The fact is, the legal marijuana market means big business for producers and sellers. Some have predicted that the marijuana industry could reach $10 billion by 2018. Many state politicians are also looking to tax the substance, realizing it could bring in much-needed revenue; just as the alcohol tax was a boon for the government after the repeal of Prohibition.

## Popular Culture

When it comes to social change, pop culture matters. Musicians from the 1960s were already extolling cannabis long before it was mainstream. Television shows such as "Mad Men," "The Office" and "Shameless" have featured characters smoking pot without it being a focus of the show.

## Influencers

With all the pieces in place, influencers have jumped in as well. More editors, journalists, and reporters are writing about cannabis as if it is something that can and should be legalized; and the probability that the national Prohibition on marijuana will end is becoming a greater reality every day.

## WHERE THE RUBBER HITS THE ROAD

With real sales and product information now available in Washington and Colorado's recreational markets, state and federal governments, as well as cannabis entrepreneurs, can get their heads around who actually consumes cannabis; in what form; and how often. For the first time, there is data on sales by product type (form factor) and consumer preferences. There'll be no more guessing, estimating, or stereotyping.

*"I think branding will be the leading trend in the industry. I can see cannabis brand loyalty becoming more of a thing as we move into the phase of states that allow for public consumption in establishments like coffee shops or cannabis bars. In those kinds of spaces, brands will be able to advertise and package their goods in more creative ways that we've yet to see. As a result, we might start noticing stronger brand loyalty in consumers because they will be in a public space happily showing off their taste preferences."*

— Brian Wansolich, Co-Founder, Leafly.com and Headset.io

Dissecting this information helps us better understand who exactly is the cannabis consumer—and the drivers that determine their product preferences and buying habits. This information—to some degree—may alleviate the "stoner" stereotypes of cannabis consumers.

This has been a long process, one where many factors have converged to transform the way we think of a substance and how some consume it. The critical next step is to deliver consistent brand cues, easy to understand brand navigation, and reliable quality products. Once legal markets are in place and managed, consumers will seek to purchase cannabis brands as they purchase widely accepted consumer brands.

As America's roughly 78 million baby boomers reach their 60s, there is no doubt that nostalgia will most likely play an even more integral role in marketing than it already does. At a time when technology is advancing at an ever-increasing pace, legendary brands and institutions from Woolworth's to Tower Records are toppling left and right. Nothing feels durable or lasting anymore. As consumers, we protectively cling to those brands that have not only endured from our childhoods but bring us back to relive the memories of that simpler, more stable time.

So, it should come as no surprise that the myriad of new cannabis brands gravitates towards that which is meaningful, aspirational, and evocative to the cannabis consumer. And according to most statistics, most cannabis consumers are just like you and me—meaning they cross all socioeconomic and racial lines. That said, it follows that cannabis products are developed much the same way that consumer-packaged goods are developed. Products are designed to bridge gaps in the market. Those markets have specific customers, and those customers have specific needs. Needs not necessarily connected to the product or even consumption of the product. This aspirational approach to marketing is how products are sold to consumers.

Canna-culture has traditionally catered to the young male smoker and his high times. Legalization has made cannabis more accessible than ever, and its application as a painkiller is particularly appealing to senior citizens. So, what does the typical cannabis consumer look like? And how do the preferences, palates, and spending habits of consumer segments, differ?

In the next chapter, we will take a closer look at the cannabis-consumer and seek to better understand consumer segments and the brand attributes that are meaningful to those groups.

## CHAPTER FIVE

# THE REAL CANNABIS CONSUMER

Who is the cannabis consumer? Despite many clichés and stereotypes, little research exists on who consumes cannabis, what form factors do they prefer, or what type of branding appeals to them. There are several relatively new firms looking into the cannabis consumer, their demographics, and purchasing habits. Headset and The Matters Group, both Seattle-based data-driven research firms are just two seeking to get a better understanding of how cannabis consumers see the world and what they want from a brand.

> *"Over the last 6+ years being within the industry I've seen a shift from generic bulk flower and edibles in plastic bags to well-designed branding and packaging efforts in line with any CPG item. Excellence in branding and packaging used to be a stand-out differentiator but with this recent trend professional branding and packaging is now baseline and expected."*
>
> *- Cy Scott, Cofounder of Leafly.com and Headset.io*

What does the typical, recreational cannabis user look like today? And how do the preferences and spending habits of groups like young men and senior citizens differ?

With the help of customer loyalty programs, Headset has created a dataset[1] of cannabis consumers based on retailer transactions enabling insight into customers' age and gender. This data was used to learn more about who buys cannabis and how they consume it. Data suggests that smokers in customer loyalty programs are overwhelmingly male, accounting for almost 70% of all participants. And, while customers range from ages 21 to 95, over 50% of loyalty participants are under 40. Headset also found that while Flower accounts for about half of the purchases made by each demographic, each group has its own specific traits. Compared to the opposite sex, men prefer concentrates and women prefer pre-rolls and edibles. Older consumers prefer edibles to pre-rolls.[2]

*"A leading trend in the cannabis industry has been the increasing involvement of women – as consumers, advocates, entrepreneurs, and investors. Women with a variety of talents are entering the space and breaking old traditions, providing a wider path for more to enter and support each other in their efforts. Gender parity isn't necessarily where it should be, but it's growing at a faster pace than has been seen in most industries, which is encouraging and a step in the right direction."*

*- Tahira Rehmatullah, President, T3 Ventures*

## Who Buys More Cannabis—Men or Women?

When Headset began their analysis, they did so by examining the customer base by gender. Are men or women more likely to visit cannabis dispensaries often? Accounting for 68.9% of customers, the ratio of men to women is well over 2:1.[3] This disparity is not surprising given cannabis culture's emphasis on the male pothead.

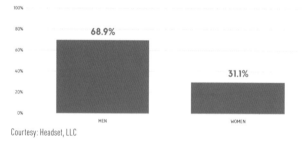

Courtesy: Headset, LLC

*"We are seeing a significant rise in the request for pre-rolls and concentrate cartridges. I attribute this to two things. First, we are serving a higher percentage of women and they are asking for discreet items such as vape pens and cartridges, as well as convenient ways to smoke flower, hence, the joints. Second, we serve a lot of tourists who are looking to consume discreetly, without having to purchase paraphernalia."*

*- Sally Vander Veer, President, Medicine Man*

## How Old Are Recreational Cannabis Users?

25-29 year-olds account for the largest percentage of customer loyalty participants (20%), followed by 21-24-year-olds (16%). Yet the average customer age is 37.6-years-old, which is older than one might expect given stereotypes about cannabis consumers. The average age for female consumers is slightly older at 38.2 while the average age for males is 37.4. People ages 65 to 95 make up less than 5% of consumers.[4]

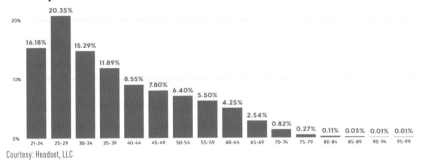

Courtesy: Headset, LLC

## How Much Money Do Consumers Spend on Cannabis?

Most consumers spend between $25 and $50 per trip to a cannabis store with a $33 median spend per trip. According to the study, 34.7% of customers spend less than $10 on average, usually picking up a single item like a half-gram pre-roll or a carbonated beverage. Only 8.2% spend more than $100/trip.[5]

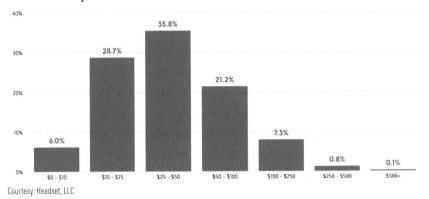

Courtesy: Headset, LLC

## How Much Money Do Consumers Spend Each Year on Cannabis?

Headset also analyzed the distribution of annual spending by customer loyalty participants. The chart below shows the total amount spent in cannabis stores over the last year by customers who have been loyalty participants for over one year.[6]

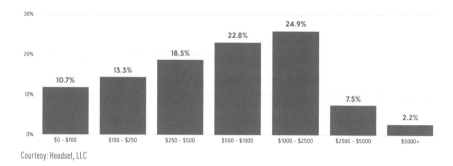

Courtesy: Headset, LLC

The median customer spends $645 on cannabis and cannabis-infused products each year, and over 57% of customers spent more than $500. Less than 10% of customers spent over $2,500.[7]

---

*"The lifting of prohibition and the explosion of information available to end-users without government or law enforcement filters is being reflected in the rapid market growth of cannabis products. No longer do cannabis users have to just smoke flower. They can now vape it, eat it and apply it topically."*

— TOM GREGORY, FOUNDER, DOSE OILS

---

## Do Different Customer Segments Have Different Shopping Habits?

To investigate, Headset first analyzed the cannabis purchasing behavior of loyalty participants by gender.

For the most part, men and women have similar shopping and spending habits. Men shop slightly more often, visiting the store about every 19.5 days compared to 21.5 days for women. Although men buy fewer items per trip, they spend almost as much ($33) as women ($35).[8]

---

*"Many of the initial products launched have targeted the regular cannabis consumer. As cannabis consumption becomes more legal and acceptable in the mainstream, the more casual consumers, often preferring a lower potency experience, come into the market. Now that a cannabis brand represents a product that is not packaged in a baggie, products and brands are not only being developed for the casual user, but also for those on the upper end of the socio-economic scale."*

— TONYA REILLY, VP, FINANCE, PRIVATEER

---

## Shopping Habits Segmented By Age

Older loyalty participants generally visit dispensaries less frequently, but they spend more when they do visit. Customers in their 80s spend the most per trip, with a median spend per trip of $64. Customers in their 40s, however, spent the most last year: a median of $823.[9]

| Customer Segment | Percent Male | Median Days Between Purchases | Median Items Per Purchase | Median Spend Per Trip | Median Spend Over Last Year |
|---|---|---|---|---|---|
| 20s | 62.1% | 16.0 | 1.6 | $27 | $627 |
| 30s | 66.2% | 18.2 | 1.7 | $33 | $677 |
| 40s | 65.3% | 20.0 | 1.9 | $39 | $823 |
| 50s | 61.6% | 20.1 | 1.8 | $41 | $753 |
| 60s | 63.9% | 26.0 | 1.8 | $43 | $552 |
| 70s | 61.6% | 22.6 | 1.6 | $50 | $165 |
| 80s + | 53.7% | 41.7 | 1.3 | $64 | N/A |

Courtesy: Headset, LLC

*"I think women and cannabis is a major trend in cannabis. I think this is the case partly because mothers have become vocal proponents of medical marijuana, and partly because we're an industry that is based on a social movement. We're not perfect, but we do take equality and fairness more seriously than most other industries."*

- EVAN NISON, FOUNDER, NISON CO.

## Do Men and Women Buy Similar Products?

Headset also looked at the popularity of particular products differed by demographic. The chart below displays the product preferences of men and women. Flower, which is "traditional" cannabis bud, is the most popular product for both genders. But it is even more popular among men: flower accounts for 4.4% more of their purchases.[10] Women tend to buy more pre-rolls and edibles, while men buy more concentrates. Women also tend to experiment more with non-traditional products (other) such as beverages, tinctures, sublinguals, and topicals.

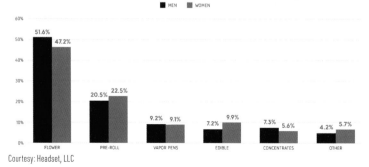

Courtesy: Headset, LLC

*"We believe that a leading trend in the industry, evidenced on the medical side and emerging on the recreational side, is the value of CBD in practical applications among many patients and recreational users, including the elderly. Being able to experience the benefits of CBD while opting out of the psychoactive effects of THC, there is a huge market for that. CBD is life-changing for a large population of people."*

*- RICK "RANGER" STEVENS, FOUNDER, JUJU JOINTS*

## Does Age Impact Product Choice?

Headset also explored product preferences by age. Each segment buys mostly Flower, with those in their 50s buying Flower at the highest rate. Older customers buy fewer Pre-Rolls than their younger counterparts. Pre-Rolls make up 27% of purchases among customers in their 20s, and this ratio drops down with each age band to only 8% of purchases for those 80 years or older.[11]

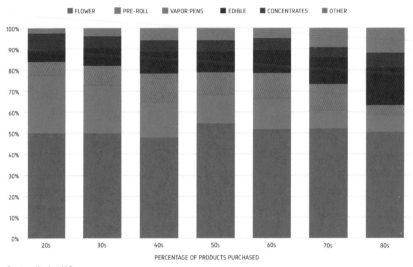

Courtesy: Headset, LLC

*"The takeaway is that today's customers want to be respected with sophisticated messaging. They want to understand the product and seek consistency in the experience. Brands more likely to realize success will utilize brand strategies that respect and educate the consumer."*

*- ERIC LAYLAND, FOUNDER, THE MATTERS GROUP*

The Matters Group qualitative survey[12] focused on respondents' worldviews such as lifestyle experience, expectations, and the drivers of their interaction and adoption of brands—believing that people who share similar worldviews are more likely to have the same opinions toward brands over people of similar demographics.

Here's what the survey set out to answer:

- What types of people will most strongly patronize a cannabis brand?
- What are the attitudes, behaviors, lifestyles, and demographic characteristics of cannabis consumers?
- What is the cannabis consumer seeking in the "ideal" cannabis brand?
- What worldviews and outlooks do these consumers want to see expressed in brands?

Approval of legalization does not equal a proclivity to consume. The study's sample revealed 71.3% generally approved of the legalization efforts in Colorado and Washington State; however, a much smaller 21.8% indicated they were at least "somewhat likely" to use cannabis products if legal in their state. As social stigmas subside and the effects of edibles are more predictable, it is expected the percentage of users to increase.[13]

---

*"As legal cannabis for adult use or medical purposes proliferates and as the stigma dissipates, an entirely new group of cannabis consumers is being created. Many entrepreneurs are focused on winning over traditional cannabis consumers from the black market, but the trend I see is the pursuit of a strategy and a brand to appeal to potential health and wellness customers who may be cannabis naive or who may have had some experience decades ago."*

— Alan J. Brochstein, Founder, 420 Investor and New Cannabis Ventures

---

## CONSUMER SEGMENTS EMERGE

Of the four groups uncovered in the study, only two are worth pursuing from a brand and marketing perspective. These segments are unique in their worldview; and while there are commonalities, they have differences in preferred brand attributes.

Survey data reveals two main "sides" in the recreational cannabis environment. Two of The Matters Group four main segments do or will patronize cannabis brands, while the remaining two do not or most likely will not.

Intriguingly, the two groups who do or would patronize cannabis brands don't always see eye to eye. Likewise, the two groups that are not interested in cannabis brands do not have a great deal in common. Each "side" of this consumer issue complicates the matter with disagreements on everything from a general worldview, including the question of cannabis's legality. It appears cannabis marketers may need to navigate issues unlike those faced in other consumer verticals. The survey's four segments provide an outline of the country's general outlook on recreational cannabis and what they want from a cannabis brand.

## The Indies

Consider themselves independent and unaligned with any political party or religious group. Think of them as relatively radical social libertarians, fierce in their self-sufficiency and servant to none. These freethinkers believe strongly in the power of the individual to live life as they want as long as they mind their own business.

Indies don't cope well with government or civic leaders, but at the same time don't need change to occur immediately. They believe they have seen much in life and don't expect real impact from the government. Not all Indies are cut from the same cloth. The group includes rich and poor, young and old. If they have one thing in common, it's an independent "to each their own" attitude.[14]

More than any other of the four segments, the Indies strongly and vocally supported the legalization of cannabis. They do and will back cannabis brands. The Indies used cannabis before it was legal and feel vindicated that the rest of the world is finally catching on. A full 28.9% of them said they would be "extremely likely" to patronize recreational cannabis if their state legalizes it.

The Indies reported they want product branding with a responsible, non-radical message. They want their preferred brands to tout what they believe to be the real benefits of cannabis, without exaggeration. Consuming to get incapacitated is not desired. Exploring, rather than escaping is the objective.

*"The increase in consumer education creates less resistance for new market opportunities that serve an increasingly more diverse demographic. These relative micro trends collectively influence the industry's democratization and, thus, normalization."*
                                                    - APRIL PRIDE, FOUNDER, VAN DER POP

## The Outsiders

Unfortunately, they feel pretty disaffected these days. Mostly in their 20s and early 30s, more female and less educated, they work hard for a middle-class income and often struggle to make ends meet. This group feels like life has stacked its deck against them, especially with coming of age in these economically challenging times. They complain a lot about the world, yet hesitate to initiate change. They see government as a cold relic, which could have something to do with their resignation.

Like Indies, Outsiders don't subscribe to religious or political groups. However, they don't think people should live however they choose. To Outsiders, life resembles a game and with prescribed right and wrongs. Unfortunately for them, playing by these rules has not given them all they feel they deserve. Others got ahead at the Outsiders expense or cut corners to climb the social ladder around this large segment.

Outsiders are an ethnically and culturally diverse group and its members are comfortable with that. They believe a greater portion of the population should share their openness to diversity. Outsiders spend more of their time engaging in outdoor activities than the other groups, including team and recreational sports such as hiking, biking, and jogging. Their households are also more likely to have at least one child.

While they have been around cannabis socially for quite some time and are comfortable with the legalization of cannabis. Outsiders may not welcome it with the enthusiasm of the Indies. That said, they don't have that kind of enthusiasm for many things.

> *"So many brands are touting "discreet" as a benefit, which is the equivalent of seeing someone drink alcohol from a brown bag, it's clandestine and hidden and therefore I consider it part of the artifacts of the war on drugs. Brands should work to rid marketing language of such artifacts of the war on drugs. Instead of discreet, easily portable or at your whim, for example."*
>
> - Pamela Johnston, SVP Strategy, Electrum Partners

## The Idealists

Younger and less wealthy than any other segment, this group is anxious. Generally, about the same size as Indies and struggles economically like Outsiders. However, they have more education and less cynicism, which makes it easier for them to believe they can affect change. They live in the present and want to influence positive change now. They feel frustrated with the current state of the country but remain hopeful that things will change for the better. They believe their current situation will improve.

They enjoy similar pursuits as the Outsider group. They both like outdoor physical activities such as team sports and individual expression. They enjoy volunteering, photography, travel, and wine tasting. These distinguished hobbies likely stem from their higher levels of education and discretionary income.

This segment agrees that the legalization of cannabis is a positive step. It reflects how they see the world. However, this support of cannabis does not extend to branded product consumption, as only 16.3% of them say they would consume branded cannabis products.[15]

---

*"Many of the new brands that are flourishing are doing so because they transcend traditional cannabis industry demographics. Sure, anyone can sell joints to millennials, but the brands that will truly take off will also draw in seniors, soccer moms, professionals, and everyone else that wants an alternative way to relax or relieve pain.*
- GRAHAM SORKIN, DIRECTOR, BUSINESS DEVELOPMENT, MARY'S MEDICINALS

---

## The Traditionalists

The only major opponents of cannabis in the study, The Traditionalist segment is older, better educated, and wealthier than the other segments. They consider themselves patriotic, structured, and self-directed. Further, they are less reckless, impetuous, progressive, and/or prone to taking a risk.

The Traditionalists don't want change, because the status quo treats them well. They believe in rules and moral order—the ones that well for them. This explains their opposition to the legalization of recreational cannabis and their unwillingness to support recreational cannabis products.[16]

*"A more educated consumer. People are now asking, where was this grown? What's the THC level? What's the terpene profile? How will this make me feel? Certain products provide a sense of euphoria or a shot of energy, while others may be perfect for a rainy day. Brands bring that consistency and comfort when making a decision. For the consumer, it's not just about getting high anymore, but a specific high to match and enhance the intended experience."*

*- MARK MCGRATH, ASSOCIATE, TUATARA CAPITAL*

## WHAT DRIVES THE CONSUMER SEGMENTS?

### The Indies: 25% Of Those Surveyed

Being advocates of legalization, Indies are comfortable with communication techniques common in other consumer verticals employed by cannabis brands. Indies are likely to consume on a more frequent basis; and as such, they are likely to vary their use of products. While smoking is the primary delivery vehicle of choice, the Indie will be among the first to try new form factors and delivery mechanisms. Indies favor fashionable, innuendo-driven, sexy, humorous, even naughty branding. They resent the "hard sell" as they choose to live life on their terms.[17]

*"With the rush to market, the products are "one bud fits all", but that is not true as we all know we have our own preferences. Marketing to minorities, specific age groups, and genders are a must. MAC Cosmetics has divisions that focus on specific groups such as Asian, Latino, and African American because each group has its own concerns and palettes. This will be the same for cannabis."*

*- OPHELIA CHONG, FOUNDER, YUN MUN*

### The Outsiders: 15% Of Those Surveyed

Outsiders may use cannabis products as an escape from their daily, disaffected life. For them, it helps leave the workday behind or celebrate the weekend. They embrace themes of affluence, fashion, sophistication, intellectualism, adventure, self-assuredness, and creativity. Those frustrating feelings towards life may point to and inform the qualities they seek in a brand. They may want that angst reflected in their brand of choice or perhaps see qualities they feel they do not possess. The survey revealed the characteristic "least" preferred by Outsiders is "Affordable" while the most preferred brand characteristic is "Affluence." The takeaway being, Outsiders don't want to be reminded of their economic challenges.[18]

## The Idealists: 23% Of Those Surveyed

Idealists represent the antithesis of the Outsiders. They are not likely to patronize cannabis brands, though they generally support legalization. According to the survey, this segment rejects every branding attribute except "Sexy" and "Organic." Advertising messages in general are viewed with skepticism.[19]

> "I see the cannabis industry is moving towards more established ways of commercializing products. Cannabis is being broken down into its component cannabinoids, concentrated, recombined with its own and other herbal ingredients, and delivered in ways that continue to move away from a smoking modality—the plant itself or its concentrates. There will always be those who wish to smoke, but the big trend is away from smoking as cannabis becomes more mainstream. There just aren't any medicinal herbs or natural remedies that are delivered to people through smoking."
> - STEVEN MARSHANK, FOUNDER, VERDUS

## The Traditionalists: 37% Of Those Surveyed

What branding would the Traditionalists prefer? None. The Traditionalist doesn't support legalization and will not patronize cannabis brands. Investing resources in an attempt to win them over would be wasteful. There may be a political rationale for communicating with this audience, but it would be a long-term effort to change the perception of cannabis legalization.[20]

## Summary

Perhaps the above is some of the first evidence that shows the diversity in cannabis consumers. Be it recreational or medicinal, there is now both quantitative and qualitative data to dispel many of the myths and stereotypes surrounding cannabis consumers.

Headset's customer loyalty data shows that there is a wide range of cannabis consumers. Each customer segment brings their own habits and product preferences with them into the cannabis store. Further, The Matter Group's study suggests and supports the notion that there are different mindsets and unique worldviews creating differences in preferences for brands and their attributes.

As the industry develops, talking generically about "pot sales" may become analogous to talking about "alcohol sales" rather than the beer, wine, and liquor categories, each segment unique and different.

Research

Strategy

Analytics

Execution

Data-Driven Marketing
For Sustainable Growth.

# Matters.

INSIGHT. AUDIENCE. RESULTS.

TheMatters.Group | 206.420.6121 | info@thematters.group

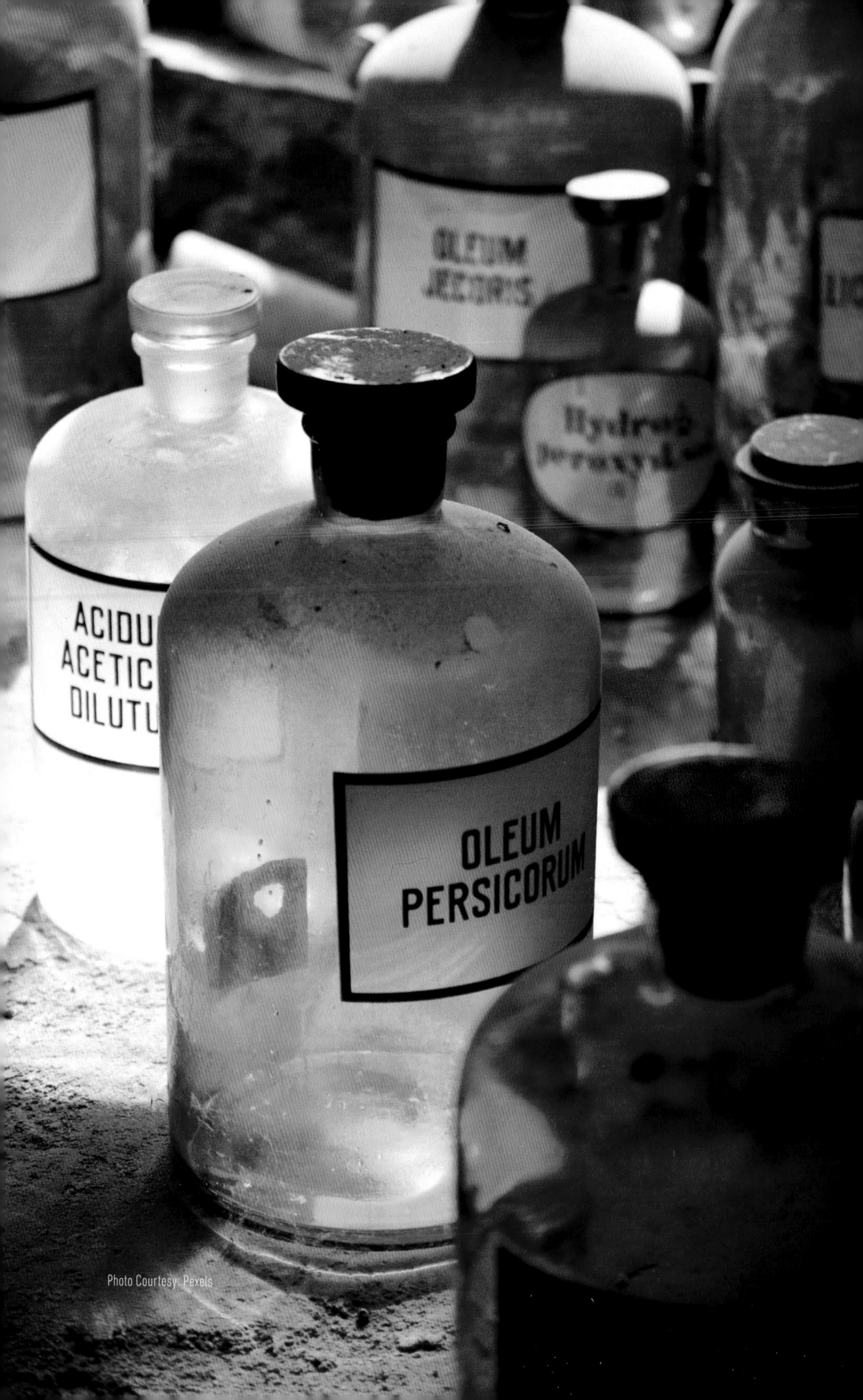


Photo Courtesy: Pexels

CHAPTER SIX

# DEVELOPING CANNABIS BRANDS

---

*"Developing cannabis brands is both an art and a science. In many ways, it's similar to developing consumer product goods—except the target keeps moving and the rules of the game keep changing. The key is finding things that are consistent and making them pillars of your brand."*

- DAVID PALESCHUCK, AUTHOR AND FOUNDER, PALESCHUCK

---

## A BRIEF OVERVIEW OF BRANDING

The mass manufacturing and marketing of the industrial revolution spurred the growth of visual identification and trademarks. It also pointed out the importance and value of visual identification systems and trademarks. Before the end of the US Civil War in 1865, bulk goods were sold by weight from barrels and open containers. These products weren't offered as "brand names" as we know them today—although some manufacturers, such as producers of tobacco, wine, and ale, did brand their trademarks onto wooden packages or casks—and still sold them as commodities. The Civil War economy created a ripe climate for technological advances and the start of a "packaged goods" society. Soldiers needed canned goods and uniforms. People began to buy ready-made clothing and shoes. More and more, people were drawn away from commodities sold out of barrels to attractively packaged goods that promised "sealed freshness" and products promising sterility and cleanliness.[1]

Courtesy: Pexels

Before the 1880s, people simply bought crackers from a cracker barrel (or any other example of an unpackaged product) and weren't aware of the manufacturer. Companies had to find ways to promote their "brand names" to customers through more earnest visual identities and attractive packaging including labels, boxes, and wrappers. At first, tobacco companies burnished their "brand names" into the wooden barrels sold to shopkeepers. Soon thereafter, medicine manufacturers and tobacco companies would lead the way with proprietary names, decorative labels, and unique packaging.[2]

The folding box enabled the cereal industry to flourish. A manufacturer put a commodity in a small box, injected "personality," added information to increase its usefulness, and turned the goods into something both desirable and extremely profitable. The success of selling packaged goods also depended on advertising the "name" yet it was something more than the name—it was the established identity of the "brand name." This brand identity differentiated the product from others of the same category and enabled buyers to appraise its value before buying.

The role of the brand name's brand mark, label, packaging, and advertising design was to stimulate sales and make the brand more desirable. Thus, it began that people wanted brand names. Names that were impressive and reliable; names they could trust for a variety of reasons, such as freshness, quality, and sanitary packaging. They wanted brands that would make their lives easier and more pleasurable; they wanted brands that would make them more attractive, socially acceptable, and desirable.

A convergence of modern factors—such as the invention of photography and typewriters, a rising literacy rate, the rise of mass media, the increase in railways, the telephone, and better postal systems—greatly facilitated the success of brands.[3]

---

*"A lot more emphasis on the branding and positioning of products, far less of the puns and stereotypical 'stoner' marketing. Companies are evolving their packaging, branding, messaging and their positioning to connect to customers on a visceral level. We are seeing brands start to stand out and bubble up to the top of the market and top of people's minds when they think about cannabis. This is just the beginning of really sophisticated branding and marketing in this industry. "*

— ADAM SMITH, FOUNDER, AVITAS

---

## The Twentieth Century

During the first twenty years of the twentieth century, America prospered. Industrial growth was great. Many people had enough income to spend some on goods, services, and luxuries.

Graphic design, advertising, and marketing stimulated the "consumer" economy. People with disposable income spent it on branded goods, from automobiles to phonographs to soft drinks.

Courtesy: Nicolò Caratelli

The rise of mass media contributed greatly to the rise of a "brand world" and the desire for brands. Radio sponsorships by brands, and later radio advertisements, paved the way for people to embrace the notion that brands could bring them happiness, both directly and indirectly. Not only would a brand name soap clean your clothes better, but it also paid for a broadcast radio program that was entertaining.

Television would be the next big venue for brands. Imitating radio marketing, brand names sponsored television programming and later paid for television commercial spots. Besides the brand identities created for consumer goods and services, it was the identification systems for corporations that set certain standards for the creation of all identification systems, comprehensive programs that went far beyond the design of a logo or trademark. A cohesive image created by a unified,

Photo Courtesy: Chris Benson

consistent, professional visual communication program was the goal. Brand identity gave a corporation a "look," a style, an image, and personality.

Consumers may look at branding as an aspect of products or services, as it often serves to denote a certain attractive quality, characteristic, or brand promise. From the perspective of brand owners, branded products or services can command higher prices. Where two products resemble each other, but one of the products has no associated branding (generic, for example,), people may often select the more expensive branded product based on the perceived quality of the brand or the basis of the reputation of the brand owner.

> *"Cannabis is an experience, whether growing or consuming. The brands that will succeed are the ones that will provide an experience from the moment a consumer engages with their product."*
>
> — GLACE BONDESON, DOPE MAGAZINE

## BRANDING AND BRAND IDENTITY

Branding is a disciplined process used to build awareness and extend customer loyalty. It requires a mandate from the top and readiness to invest in the future. Branding is about seizing every opportunity to express why people should choose one brand over another. A desire to lead, outpace the competition, and give employees the best tools to reach customers are the reasons why companies leverage branding.[4]

Brand identity is tangible and appeals to the senses. You can see it, touch it, hold it, hear it, watch it move. Brand identity fuels recognition, amplifies differentiation and makes big ideas and meaning accessible. Brand identity takes disparate elements and unifies them into whole systems including but not limited to name, logo, tagline/catchphrase, graphics, shapes, colors, sounds, scents, tastes, and movements.[5]

Photo Courtesy: F. Stopp

## Visual Brand Identity

The recognition and perception of a brand are highly influenced by its visual presentation. A brand's visual identity is the overall look of its communications. Effective visual brand identity is achieved by the consistent use of particular visual elements to create distinction, such as specific fonts, colors, and graphic elements. At the core of every brand identity is a brand mark, or logo. In the United States, brand identity and logo design naturally grew out of the modernist movement of the 1950s and greatly drew on the principles of that movement—simplicity and geometric abstraction.

## Brand Trust and Expanding The Role Of Brand

Over time, brands came to embrace a performance or benefit promise, for the product, certainly, but eventually also for the company behind the brand. Today, brand plays a much bigger role. Brands have been co-opted as powerful symbols in larger debates about economics, social issues, and politics. The power of brands to communicate a complex message quickly with emotional impact and the ability to attract media attention, make them ideal tools for executing branding strategies.

## How Brands Use Color to Educate, Evoke Emotion and Convey Efficacy

Color is a particularly important element of visual brand identity and color mapping provides an effective way of ensuring color contributes to differentiation in a visually cluttered marketplace. Most shoppers—93 percent of them—make purchase decisions based on color and visual appearance. With a statistic like that, cannabis brand owners are spending time and money selecting the right colors for their logos, packaging, websites, and other brand assets in the race for buyers' attention—the cannabis consumer.[6]

Photo Courtesy: Minimalist

## The Science Behind Color and Emotion

Color resonates with people in different ways. We all have a favorite. That said, the color used by brands says a lot about the brand itself. The science behind our emotional connections to color is complicated, but it is becoming more evident through anecdotal knowledge and scientific experimentation.

Is it possible that our brains are wired to like (or dislike) certain colors? It all relates to emotional responses when we see (a) color. A study by researchers at Wellesley College,[7] *Neural Basis For Unique Hues* links neural processes to color. It further relates some of the things we already know, such as that color context changes based on other colors in the field of vision, and emotion is a big factor when thinking about color.

## Color Impacts Intuition

Color research is not a new phenomenon. It can be traced to works that are hundreds of years old. One of the most relevant today remains *"Theory of Colors"*[8] by Johann Wolfgang von Goethe, which was first published in 1810. While this was not a "scientific work" per se, it set the course for much of what we know about color and the basis for future research.

Goethe published one of the first color wheels and associated color with more than hue; he also revealed color's psychological impact. His theory about how color impacts our emotions and thoughts is still widely used and applies to how we think about color. The book is a great read for anyone with an interest in color theory.

The truth of the matter is that color is too dependent on personal experiences to be universally translated to specific feelings. Research shows that it's likely because elements such as personal preference, experiences, upbringing, cultural differences, and context often muddy the effect individual colors have on us.[9]

There are broader messaging patterns to be found in color perceptions. For instance, colors play a fairly substantial role in purchases and branding. In an appropriately titled Study called, *"Impact of Color in Marketing,"*[10] researchers found that up to 93 percent of snap judgments made about products can be based on color alone, depending on the product.[11]

Regarding the role that color plays in branding, results from studies show that the relationship between brands and color hinges on the perceived appropriateness of the color being used for the particular brand.

The study *"Exciting Red And Competent Blue"*[12] also confirms that purchasing intent is greatly affected by colors due to the impact they have on how a brand is perceived. This means that colors influence how consumers view the "personality" of the brand in question.

Additional studies have revealed that our brains prefer recognizable brands, which makes color incredibly important when creating a brand identity. It has even been suggested that it is of paramount importance for new brands to specifically target logo colors that ensure differentiation from entrenched competitors (if the competition all uses blue, brands will stand out by using purple).[13]

Certain colors do broadly align with specific traits, such as brown with ruggedness and red with excitement. Nearly every academic study on colors and branding will conclude that it is far more important for a brand's colors to support the personality it wants to portray instead of trying to align with stereotypical color associations.

> *"If the consumer isn't convinced the endorsement and/or connection is authentic, it may affect the brand undesirably. Further, if a consumer doesn't believe the celebrity actually uses or supports the brand they're endorsing, it will have an adverse effect on the brand."*
> - Mia Willmott, Artist

## Logo Color Effects Consumer Habits

"The specific colors used in a company's logo have a significant impact on how that logo, and the brand as a whole, is viewed by consumers," according to a study conducted by researchers at the University of Missouri-Columbia. The study found specific links and ties to colors within logos and how people felt about those brands.

The findings change some of the ideas that we associate with specific colors. "Of all the feelings associated with logo colors, the feelings associated with red logos were the most surprising," wrote one researcher. "Traditional emotions based on red include aggression and romance, but red logos did not invoke those emotions in study participants. This can probably be attributed to the fact that red is used in logos of many well-established brands such as State Farm, McDonald's, and Coca-Cola, so consumers have pre-existing emotions associated with brands using that color."[14]

> *"One of the leading trends in the cannabis industry right now is sleek, minimalist branding. This is part of the broader trend of "shedding the stoner stigma." New businesses want to get away from the counter-cultural image of an illicit drug. I think this trend will die down once cannabis consumers are less stigmatized (which is already happening). Positioning a brand as above "stoners" only fuels the negative stereotype."*
> - Monah Zhang, Author, Heard On The Tree

## Beyond Red, Yellow, and Green

How are cannabis brands using color in their logos and marketing materials to differentiate themselves from the crowd? While many have followed the expected and stereotypical path, others have consciously thought through their color palette, brand essence, and strategy.

Not surprising is that most new cannabis brands use blue and green tones and shades more than any other colors. Some brands—such as Mary's Medicinals—intentionally use black and white exclusively to differentiate themselves. Others use visual cues and anchors that we associate with the history of cannabis such as tie-dye or the red, yellow, and green of Rastafarianism.

Photo Courtesy: Paolo Ghedini

More typical uses of color are in the scales defining Indica versus Sativa used to denote the efficacy of a cannabis strain. Typically, colors span from dark greens, blues, and purples on the Indica side to yellows, oranges, and reds on the Sativa side, representing the restful, mellowing effects of Indica strains and the uplifting, energetic results from Sativa strains.

Mixing color, science and emotion can be a tricky game, and while science is teaching packaging designers and consumers more every day, it's also opening up more questions about how we see and feel about color and accordingly about the brands that use certain colors to convey their brand essence. If the data is correct, brands will continue to use color to appeal to their consumers' desires, as well as conscious and unconscious affinities.

*"People in the industry are trying to change the way others perceive cannabis; to educate and inform those that have a negative perception about it. The marketing and branding effort toward that end has to be one of the leading industry trends."*
- GIA GARGANESE, LOLA LOLA CANNABIS

## BRANDING STRATEGIES

Iconic brands are defined as having aspects that contribute to consumer's self-expression and personal identity. Brands whose value to consumers comes primarily from having identity value are said to be "identity brands." Some of these brands have such a strong identity that they become more or less cultural icons, which make them "iconic brands." Examples are Apple, Nike, and Harley-Davidson. Many iconic brands include almost ritual-like behavior in purchasing or consuming the products. Four key elements to creating iconic brands are[15]:

## Necessary Conditions
The performance of the product must at least be acceptable, preferably with a reputation of having good quality.

## Mythmaking
Meaningful storytelling fabricated by cultural insiders. These must be seen as legitimate and respected by consumers for stories to be accepted.

## Cultural Contradictions
A mismatch between prevailing ideology and emergent undercurrents happening in society. In other words, a difference in the way consumers are and how they wish they were.

## The Cultural Brand Management Process
Actively managing the myth-making process in making sure the brand maintains its position as an icon.

These four key elements come together to create branding strategies that are both effective and meaningful to the brand and consumer. A sampling of brand strategies include[16]:

## Aspirational and Lifestyle Branding
Aspirational branding is the strategy conveying a larger feeling, not necessarily connected to the product or consumption of the product. Brands and strategies that are considered 'aspirational' include Nike, Apple, and Patagonia, among others. Perhaps one of the best examples of aspirational branding is Jose Cuervo's *"Most Interesting Man In The World."*

## Generic and No Brand Branding
Several companies have successfully pursued "no-brand" strategies by creating packaging that imitates generic brand simplicity. Examples include the Japanese company Muji, which means "no label" in English (literally, "no-brand quality goods"). Although there is a distinct Muji brand, Muji products are not branded. This no-brand strategy means that little is spent on advertisement or classical mar-

keting. Muji's success is attributed to word-of-mouth and a simple shopping experience.

## Whimsical and Other Worldly Branding

Described as spontaneously fanciful or playful brands, these brands take an approach that includes fantasy, humor, exploration, and escape. Examples of whimsical gaming brands and titles include Candy Crush, Tapjoy, and Minecraft.

## Social Media Branding

Social media brands may be the most evolved version of the brand form because they focus on their users. In so doing, social media brands are arguably more charismatic, in that consumers are compelled to spend time with them because the time spent is on fundamental human drivers related to belonging and individualism. In essence, these brands mirror our families, our friends, our lives, and ourselves.

## Destination and Culture Branding

Destination branding used to be the work of cities, states, and other localities to promote themselves. Nowadays, it's bigger and deeper than that. A perfect example is Jamaica—and of course, Bob Marley. Destinations and the people, food, culture, and habits from that destination are all part of the package.

## Nostalgia Branding

Nostalgia branding and marketing is a perennial and wildly successful strategy by which brands resurrect the sights, sounds, and feel of a previous time to sell us a product of today. Sometimes it's by reviving a type of commercial or a style of packaging, icon, or spokesperson that guarantees fond recollection and memories. Clever companies know that the older we get, the more intense our longings for the past become. They also know that our preferences for music, movies, trends, and products we enjoyed in our carefree childhoods, adolescence, and early 20's remain with us our whole lives.

Most marketers understand the past is always better than the present. Quite simply, it is how our brains are hard-wired. It's one of the nicer functions our brain performs, as it protects us from painful memories and instills in us an everlasting optimism. But the danger, of course, is that it also makes us unwitting consumers for anything that reminds us of being young from classic dolls to retro-designed cars. And scarier still, sometimes all it takes is a subtle, subconscious cue like a few bars of an old song; old-fashioned lettering, or a picture of a dead movie idol or rock star.

---

*"Luxury and celebrity endorsements are everywhere right now in cannabis branding. They are attractive because they seem to lend credibility to an industry coming out of the shadows. But will they last to become the household names of 5-10 years forward? That remains to be seen."*

— KENNY MORRISSON, CO-FOUNDER, VCC BRANDS

---

## Post-Prohibition Branding

In much the same way as post-Prohibition alcohol brands were created, so too are post-Prohibition (legal) cannabis brands taking form. From entrepreneurs rushing in to stake their claim and those already "in the business" now coming out of the darkness, like their bootlegging predecessors, they seek to create products that are differentiated either by their taste, efficacy, consistency, or shelf appeal.

Some credit Prohibition for creating the habit of requesting liquor by brand. Supposedly, before Prohibition, when liquor was legal, people ordered their gin, scotch, or whiskey from the bartender without specifying a brand name. During this time, there were no guarantees about what came in the bottle—poison, colored water, or wood alcohol. Accordingly, people started ordering by the brand to ensure quality. Of course, that didn't ensure any such thing, but it was an attempt at getting to better, more consistent quality.

At the end of the 14-year Prohibition period, a dormant beverage industry faced considerable challenges. How could it ramp up production to satisfy demand? What exactly was that demand? And how do the current tastes and trends relate to product desirability? These are the same questions facing cannabis brands today.

---

*"The emergence of companies that have been "in hiding" for years is evident. With the rise of the recreational cannabis industry, companies need to brand themselves accordingly and establish a spot in the consumer's evoked mindset. You can either stay in the shadows and get surpassed by others coming to the light or gear up and make sure your company is at the forefront of this movement."*

—ERIC ERLANDSEN, DOPE MAGAZINE

---

# WHAT SHOULD A CANNABIS BRAND STAND FOR?

## Speaking To The Indie

Indies accept cannabis. For many, it is a part of their lives. Whether through regular consumption or vocal support for legalization, the Indie is very comfortable with messages about cannabis. In their mainstream world, common branding communication techniques are quite accepted. Creatively using the brand messages that they favored will lead to greater adoption and profitable market segments.[17]

While Indies prefer a more affordable product, they also show a fondness for cannabis products portrayed as fashionable. Indies consider themselves "aficionados." These are your influencers and tastemakers. Being "advanced" users, Indies can appreciate a more technical interaction with a brand. Communicating different "effects" and nuances between strains is appreciated. Their vocal support for legalization and higher consumption rates underscore their desire to associate with a fashionable product but also one that acknowledges their understanding of cannabis.[18]

---

*"In my opinion, it is this similarity with the wine industry that will act as a bridge between the old culture of cannabis and the emergence of new users who will want to try it now that cannabis is legal. Just as wine has its own vocabulary surrounding flavors, tannins, mouthfeel, and aroma that defines a particular wine varietal—so too does cannabis. The emergence of "cannasseurs" and "weed snobs" is a real thing and represents the most exciting demographic for growth of our industry."*

*- ERIC GASTON, OWNER THE EVERGREEN MARKET*

---

The desired quality relating to localism could be emphasized in several ways. Think of the local food trends and associated positive regional qualities. In some food and beverage verticals, the notion of 'location' has been elevated to a brand in itself. Think recognized viticultural regions such as Napa for wine, Cascade Hops in brewing, and of course Kentucky bourbon.

Relative to product naming, the Indies prefer those that are non-provocative. Their preference is for a relaxed mellow-sounding brand name. They want it to be non-offensive and non-excessive. The Indies often mentioned "nice and easy," which connotes a sensation of relaxation.

What came through was a rejection of "whimsical" names. The Matters Group analysis revealed a desire of Indies and their love for cannabis to be treated with respect. They tend to avoid "stoner stereotypes" and want brands to present themselves in a manner in line with the newly established legitimacy of cannabis.

## Speaking To The Outsider

Outsiders represent the largest contingent of The Matters Group Survey. A sizable 72.1 percent of Outsiders agreed with legalization, yet when asked about the use of recreational cannabis if it were available in their state, only 26.3 percent stated they were "somewhat" or "extremely" likely to consume. Additionally, they are not likely to be vocal advocates or consumers. Not only do they feel "outside" of mainstream society, but they are also a quiet majority on the legalization of cannabis. Cannabis has been in their lives to some degree and is, therefore, somewhat neutral.[19]

---

*"A leading trend in the cannabis industry today can be seen in the 'premium' value proposition of many cannabis flower and concentrate brands. Aligning closely to the small-batch premium brand story of 'limited availability' that has been seen as a major value driver of the wine and spirits industries over the past decade, scarcity in this infant marketplace of otherwise like products has and will continue to successfully capture the 'top-shelf' across many legal markets."*

- MATTHEW ANDERSON, PARTNER - MACARTHUR CAPITAL, LLP

---

The typical Outsider prefers aspirational brands relative to their place in society. They appreciate brands that espouse affluence, fashion, sophistication, intellect, adventure, self-assuredness, and creativity. The Outsiders certainly have these qualities, but within the context of their worldview, the most desirable brand attributes are those they do not see in their current life situation. This returns us to our presumption that the Outsiders who do use cannabis, do so as an escape mechanism. Brands strategically positioned as aspirational and delivering an experience of escaping the daily routine will connect with the Outsider's desires.[20]

---

*"Brands strategically positioned as aspirational and delivering an experience of escaping the daily routine will connect with the Outsider's desires."*

- ERIC LAYLAND, THE MATTERS GROUP

---

This group is socially responsible and wants brands to avoid "immaturity" or "recklessness." And while many consume cannabis products for fun, they prefer responsibility in their brand's messaging. They desire sophisticated and mature product positioning.

The Survey showed there is an overwhelming rejection of historical stereotypes. For today's emerging cannabis consumer, the past is the past. The new reality portrays products as positive and upscale but not out of reach. Again, the strongest indexed attributes for Outsiders were affluence, fashion, sophistication, intellect, adventure, confidence, and creativity. This influential and lucrative segment is demanding and will vote with their wallets.[21]

*"Selling a product line with strain variations of Indica, Sativa or CBD casts a wider consumer net. However, the way a product is going to actually affect someone has countless variables ranging from the time of day the product was consumed and/or even the bodyweight of the consumer. Consider a strain like Durban Poison; maybe it's your favorite strain and we think we understand how Durban Poison affects us. However, will the same strain by a different grower give us the same experience? Now multiply that Durban Poison by multiple growers utilizing the Durban Poison by different extraction methods. Will Durban Poison in a flower form affect us the same as a concentrate? Exactly how different is Durban Poison from other sticky Sativas? Or is the strain name a marketing ploy to get the consumer to notice the product? I think this will be a mystery for a long time."*

*- Jamie Hoffman, Founder, Craft Elixirs*

## WHAT DOES THIS MEAN FOR CANNABIS BRANDS?

According to the Survey, there are two consumer segments to focus on when developing a brand and bringing it to market. The Indie and Outsiders comprise the most targetable and profitable audiences for cannabis brands. Together they comprise 59 percent of the legal-age general population. They overlap in worldview and brand attributes, but nuanced strategies should be executed for maximum brand adoption. Idealists consume cannabis; however, given their resistance to brand messaging, significant investments to attract this audience may not reap the rewards of other segments.[22]

*"Brands are working hard to help consumers navigate to the products and information they need. Most shoppers, especially those new to cannabis, need cues to help guide them through a fragmented and evolving marketplace. By addressing specific consumers, their needs and wants, and their preferences and perspectives, brands are creating more access to the benefits of cannabis."*

- ELIZABETH HOGAN, VP, BRAND AND COMMUNICATIONS, WILLIE'S RESERVE

Much of the effort in strategic brand development occurs well before creative execution. Though it's easy to get energized by brainstorming visual concepts. Developing a brand involves much more than a color pallet, logo, and slogan. It is an emotional response triggered by a trust established between the brand and the consumer. The foundation for trust begins with understanding needs and desires and delivering a supportive experience.

Products begin with addressing consumer's unmet needs. Brands connect with the target audiences by communicating the qualities the consumer seeks and how the product can deliver. Brand execution continuously reinforces the appropriate product qualities including, but not limited to positioning, naming, packaging, pricing, availability, advertising, messaging, user experience, and service.

*"Having developed several cannabis brands, I've found that every project has a set of evolving hurdles to navigate. From company to company, product to product, or state to state, there are constant changes to rules and regulations that must be considered when developing a cannabis brand. It's like building a train while it's rolling down the tracks."*

- MIQ WILLMOTT, ARTIST

Successful brands pay close attention to all the consumer touchpoints. They make a promise to consumers and consistently fulfill that promise with each interaction.

The takeaway is that when naming brands, reflecting desired attributes is more likely to lead to a favorable response in consumers. Brand names that evoke harder drug use or that do not convey elements of the user experience will have a more difficult time gaining widespread acceptance by the Indie and Outsider segments.

CHAPTER SEVEN

# CANNABIS COMMERCIALIZATION

Among the variety of ways cannabis can be consumed, smoking and oral consumption are most common. Each method leads to slightly different psychoactive effects due to the activation and passage of THC and other component chemicals. It is generally considered that smoking—which includes toxins created by combustion—produces a somewhat more relaxing effect while eating delays the onset of effect and the duration typically longer.[1]

Patients and recreational consumers alike are increasingly moving away from the typical means of consumption (smoking) to other methods for both reasons of health and discretion. Stigmas remain for smoking anything and cannabis in general. These new form factors provide discrete use and a broader appeal to cannabis connoisseurs and potential consumers alike.

---

*"Cannabis mirrors the food industry very closely with respect to the growth of supply chains on a national scale. Consumers and regulators will call attention to food safety in edibles after the inevitable fallout of a major recall due to foodborne illness. We will also see a focused lens on safety in cultivation involving pest management and testing for contaminants. Building brand loyalty and trust requires a foundation of safety and quality."*

- AARON BIOS, EDITOR/PUBLISHER, MARIJUANA INDUSTRY JOURNAL

---

## MEANS OF INGESTION AND FORM FACTOR

While cannabis research has been constrained in the U.S. over the past few decades, we are now rapidly learning about the wide-reaching therapeutic effects of cannabis and how the plant's cannabinoid compounds react with our endocannabinoid system. There are four key uptake systems from which the body can absorb cannabinoids.

### Inhalation of Cannabis

The traditional way to intake THC is to smoke it, which generally provides a rapid onset of euphoria and other therapeutic effects within five to ten minutes. Vaporization is also popular, as vaporized cannabis provides the rapid onset of relief without the potentially harmful carcinogens related to smoking.

When you inhale cannabis, the majority of cannabinoids, enter the body through the lungs, where they are passed along directly into your bloodstream. Due to this direct exchange, consuming cannabis via inhalation has the shortest time of effect of all routes of uptake.

From a health standpoint, a comparison of smoked cannabis to vaporization reveals that their potential advantages associated with vaporization which includes more efficient cannabinoid extraction and higher THC/CBD levels within concentrates including oil, wax, rosin, and shatter—and a decreased exposure to toxic elements such as carbon monoxide and tar created when smoking.

### Ingestion

In addition to inhalation, cannabis can be consumed orally. Affectionately known as edibles, cannabis consumed orally enters the bloodstream after being broken down in the stomach and absorbed in the intestines.

Cannabis-infused foods and liquids take extra time to break down because they pass through the gastrointestinal tract and liver before entering the bloodstream. The experience of consuming cannabis-infused foods can feel much different than inhaling cannabis because when cannabis is ingested in a solid or liquid form, a potent THC metabolite

(11-hydroxy THC) forms in the liver. This metabolite has a higher affinity to bind to cannabinoid receptors and is five to ten times more psychoactive than the originally ingested THC. Edible products can take from thirty minutes to two hours to take effect and can result in varying levels of psychoactive effects depending on several variables —including dosage, what and how much has been previously eaten; a tolerance to cannabis, among others.[2]

### Sublingual/Oral-Mucosal:

One of the most efficient ways to absorb THC and other cannabinoids is through the mucosal lining of the mouth. Within the mouth, three areas absorb cannabis: the mucosal lining inside the entire mouth; the area under the tongue (sublingual); and the tongue itself. Common examples of medications include dissolvable strips, sublingual sprays, or medicated lozenges, or tinctures.

Cannabis products placed under the tongue (sublingually) take effect more quickly than those absorbed through the general mucosal tissue lining the mouth or placed on the tongue itself. With this uptake method, the effects of cannabis should be felt in fifteen minutes to one hour.

### Transdermal

Cannabinoids, much like the active ingredients in other medications, can also be absorbed through the skin. Examples of topical products include creams, balms, and even patches similar to those used to quit smoking cigarettes.

While not widely studied, there is research that shows that topical application of cannabinoids has an onset of action within minutes locally (i.e. creams and balms applied to the skin), with the duration of these effects lasting one to two hours. Individuals who used patches reported onset of action within two hours and duration of effect lasting upwards of two days.[3]

Cannabis-infused topicals (lotion, balms, and soaks) readily enter the skin layers only. They're effective at relieving pain and inflammation in the area in which they're applied.

Since cannabinoids don't enter the bloodstream with this intake method, topically applied THC has doesn't have the opportunity to cross the blood-brain barrier (unless applied internally), and thus has no psychoactive properties. Topicals offer a fast-acting localized effect and have been known to help reduce scarring and may help with psoriasis/eczema.[4]

## Discretion Drives Move To New Forms Of Consumption

According to a Headset's report,[5] both Millennials (under 35) and the Silent Generation (76 and older) are leading the way in the movement toward discretion.[6] Although on opposites of the demographic spectrum, both age groups are discovering different ways to enjoy or medicate. Less than half (47 percent) of cannabis purchased by Millennials and older consumers is flower, highlighting the shift to newer forms of consumption.

But it's not just younger and older Americans making the switch. Generation X (ages 35-53) and Baby Boomers (ages 54-75) are also hopping aboard the discretion bandwagon. Gen-Xers spend 55 percent of their cannabis dollars on flower and Boomers spend 59 percent on flower. But that leaves a huge chunk of the retail market open for innovative new products.[7]

The data, although not totally surprising given the rapid development of a growing marketplace, suggests that discerning cannabis consumers are searching for less overt and potentially more healthy options.

*"As the industry matures and the market reacts to consumers' actual needs, there is a sea change in consumption habits. This is what the mainstreaming of marijuana looks like."*

*- David Rheins, Founder and Executive Director, MJBA*

For the older generation of consumers, cannabis capsules are the second most popular form factor after flower at eleven percent.[8] Edibles, topicals, and tinctures are also more in vogue for the senior set. For the Millennial crowd, concentrates and oil accounts for nearly a quarter of all purchases. Vape pens are popular among all demographic groups.

The "discretion trend" highlighted by Headset validates other data suggesting that it is older Americans who are creating the market shift in marijuana consumption trends. A recent report reveals that seniors are far outpacing teen cannabis in both consumption and the adoption of new forms of ingestion.

A study from the CDC (Centers for Disease Control) showed that those who said they'd used cannabis in the prior month grew 455 percent among those aged 55 to 64, and 333 percent for those 65 and over. It dropped 10 percent for 12-to-17-year-olds during the same period.[9]

## A LOOK AT CURRENT LEGAL CANNABIS BRANDS

Having called out the means of cannabis consumption and legal form factors currently available to cannabis consumers in the US—let's take a look at some of the current U.S. cannabis products, brands, and packaging.

# CANNABIS FLOWER

## Cannabis Flower

When people think about cannabis, they most often think about smoking it. Throughout history and even to this day, smoking remains the most popular method of consumption. Cannabis can be smoked with implements such as bongs, hookahs, and pipes. Makeshift pipes or commercial pipes may be used, or cigarette-like joint or cigar-like blunt may be smoked. Local methods have differed by the preparation of the cannabis plant before use, the parts of the cannabis plant that are used, and the treatment of the smoke before inhalation. In early times, as in some parts of Africa today, a pile of cannabis was simply laid on fire and the smoke inhaled.[10]

As cannabis consumption is rising, cannabis flower is declining as a percentage of total cannabis sales.[11] That said, it still makes up more than sixty percent of sales nationally and more than seventy percent of sales in many key markets,

Photo Courtesy: Erik Hecht

including California. This is largely due to the continued support for flower by heavy consumers (those who consume at least five times per week). Seventy percent of heavy consumers report using flower, compared with less than forty percent of moderate and occasional users.[12] Many heavy users purchase both flower and other products such as edibles and concentrates.

*"Curing is almost as important as growing. Practicing responsible growing and production practices is very important to our company. Dawg Star seeks to grow via sustainable methods and practices. Growing indoors uses a great deal of energy, so we're expanding to greenhouses and outdoor facilities to reduce energy use. No plastic bags or harmful chemicals as we grow as clean as possible. In the end, our team treats the plant with respect and provides high quality, tested products."*

*- TREK MANZONI, CO-FOUNDER, DAWG STAR*

Photo Courtesy: Dawg Star

Flower, also called "bud," refers to the smokable part of the cannabis plant that has gone through the cultivation, harvest, drying, and curing process. Flower continues to be a popular choice for its simplicity and versatility, offering numerous methods of consumption, such as being smoked using a pipe or bong, or by rolling it into a joint or blunt.

Among the many benefits of smoking flower, is its rapid onset. Flower's high bioavailability means its effects are felt almost instantaneously.

*"High-quality products must be a priority for all cannabis companies. What will differentiate one great product from the next is the company's brand identity and marketing. All cannabis business at this stage is small business; market share is up for grabs. With that said, the people and families currently in the cannabis industry only have a handful of years before big business makes their presence*

*felt. It's important to think big in these upcoming years while focusing on all of the intermediate goals and little details that'll get you there."*

— Charlie Cassidy, Co-Founder, TKO Reserve

Photo Courtesy: IVXX

"It's becoming more and more commonplace for people to recognize the huge variability that exists between products and brands. This is especially true for cannabis flower, where natural biological variation plus different growing conditions between growers yields flower with different effects. People are becoming more aware that the Indica vs. Sativa distinction, and even strain identities, are minimally predictive of the experience the consumer will have. Products with consistent chemical profiles will become more and more popular because consumers want a consistent, reliable experience. In terms of flower, I think that the Indica vs. Sativa distinction, and even strain designations, will eventually be replaced by more rigorous classification schemes that come from carefully measuring the unique chemical profile of each batch of flower grown."

— Nick Jikomes, Ph.D. Senior Science Advisor, Leafly

## Marley Natural

Photo Courtesy: Marley Natural

*"A key trend in cannabis continues to point toward brand and trust, in a market where few precedents of standard practice have been established. From a marketing perspective, this is obtained with a clear foundation of values and principles—elements that must be adhered to in the brand message, and which match the product and the people behind it."*

*- Tracy Anderson, Former Marketing Director, Marley Natural and Co-Founder, Pure Beauty*

### Solstice

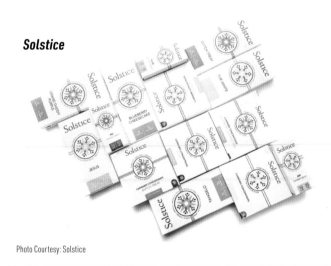

Photo Courtesy: Solstice

*"Early on we've seen packaging aesthetics largely inspired by the stoner culture - pot leaves, funky mascots, and every shade of green you can imagine. But we've always drawn inspiration from the opportunity to change perception—hence the name Solstice. Cannabis isn't just for people who fit the stereotype, and that mantra continues to push us to design products that would look at home on any shelf—not just pot shops."*

*- Will Denman, Co-Founder, Solstice*

### Saints Joints

Impeccably designed, the branding elements consist of colorful artist-designed collectible pull-tab boxes created by well-known artists including Jimbo Phillips, Skinner, and Jeremy Fish. Saints Joints pays close attention to the details starting with the flower and consistent grind to the branded custom cones for a consistent and stylish burn.

Photo Courtesy: Saints Joints
(Artist Collaboration: Caitlin Mattison and Alan Forbes)

"Cannabis, like any other consumable good is about connecting with the consumer and creating a unique experience. We focus on every product detail with a keen eye on the two most important elements: our flower and our packaging. One grabs your attention and the other keeps you coming back. Our partnerships with artists, influencers, and cultivators have resulted in limited editioned designed boxes created by well-known artists including, Skinner, Jimbo Phillips, Jeremy Fish, among others."

— LAWRENCE PERRIGO, FOUNDER, SAINTS JOINTS

### Lola Lola

Lola Lola's new product line showcases the unique ability of cannabis strains to enhance specific activities and moods, Their experiential icons and intensity color spectrum make it simple to pinpoint the right product for each occasion. Lola Lola's line range includes healing CBD products through hash-infused psychoactive products.

Photo Courtesy: Lola Lola

"I would have to say that the people in the industry are trying to change the way others perceive cannabis; to educate and inform those that have a negative perception about cannabis. The marketing and branding aspect of the industry is changing tremendously and has to be one of the leading trends. While talking to many people at conferences and cannabis shows about the direction we see the industry going, it seems that everyone is trying to get the stereotypical 'stoner' 'lazy' 'couch potato' vibe out of the way and inform others that it is much more than that and is truly a magical plant."

— GIA GARGANESE, LOLA LOLA

Photo Courtesy: Western Cultured

"Terpenes and strains are the leading trends in the industry and we here at Western Cultured believe it's just the beginning of a trend that is here to stay, becoming a backbone of cannabis education and understanding. Terpenes are naturally occurring molecules that give all flowers aroma and flavor. The terpene and cannabinoid profiles of each strain are capable of creating unique experiences, much the same way smells of food or perfume evoke different sensations."

*- BRIANNA HUGHES, FOUNDER, WESTERN CULTURED*

*Trinity*

Photo Courtesy: Nelson Miyazaki

"New products are embracing the gender, age, lifestyle, and economic breadth of their customer base and branding themselves appropriately. For designers, this means we are no longer boxed in by cannabis clichés or catch-all solutions. We get to show the power of design thinking—how articulating the product's goals, analyzing the market landscape, and narrowing in on a target audience can lead to the creation of brands that truly resonate with consumers."

*- BILLI KID, ARTIST AND DESIGNER*

# Terpene Education
## Flavor & aroma of cannabis

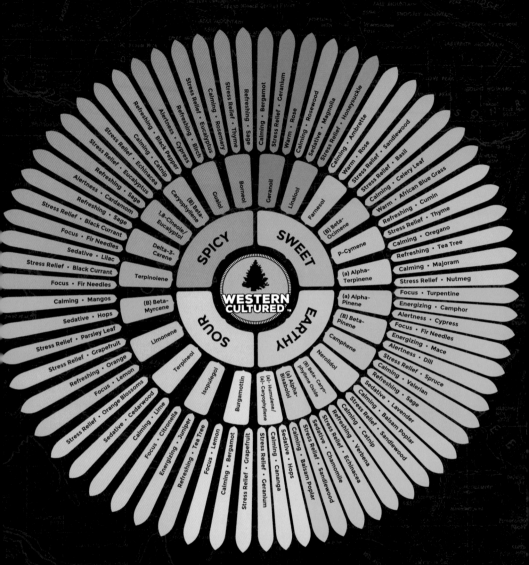

Pungent organic compounds made by a variety of plants to attract pollinators or avert predators in nature. Over 100 different types of terpenes have been found in cannabis, each strain having a unique composition. The full interaction of all cannabinoid & terpene compounds within the body's endocannabinoid system after cannabis is inhaled or ingested is known as the "entourage effect". The individual terpene profile in each strain influences the "high" one experiences due to the synergy/intercommunication of the compounds in that flower. Terpenes are fragile so to prevent degradation of your cannabis, store in a cool & dark place.

# LIGHT UP THE MOMENT™
## WESTERNCULTURED.COM

Photo Courtesy: Nelson Miyazaki

### Pr%ff

"Proofing" started as a way of protecting consumers as they traded whiskey during the 18th century. The parallels between alcohol prohibition in the 1920s and the continued prohibition of cannabis in modern society are strikingly similar. A perfect example of a tongue-in-cheek brand relating the prohibition of alcohol to that of cannabis.

### Firetruck

"Comin' In Hot" is this Seattle-based high testosterone novelty brand's catchphrase. The matchbook w/ match-strike package comes complete with two half gram pre-rolls, two matches, and a sticker to boot.

Photo Courtesy: Nelson Miyazaki

Photo Courtesy: Sitka

### Sitka

Sitka was perhaps one of the few to start the micro-dosing trend when it comes to pre-rolls. While most go smaller, Sitka chose to create medium potency cannabis delivered in a cigarette-like cylinder rather than the more typical cone.

### Leafs By Snoop

Leafs By Snoop cannabis products are made under a Colorado marijuana license belonging to Beyond Broadway, which does business as LivWell and will grow all of the brand's flower and manufacture its edibles and concentrates.

Photo Courtesy: Leafs By Snoop

Photo Courtesy: Dawg Star

### Dawg Star

Dawg Star, Seattle's first licensed producer, manufacturers some of the best cannabis and derivatives including flower and concentrates. The Pyramid Pack is Dawg Star's answer to convenient, quality pre-rolls.

> *"Cannagars are a new luxury category the industry is now starting to enjoy. With few established brands available, demand is high for a quality cannagar that expresses and exudes luxury. I envision a luxury cannabis culture that parallels the elite VIP lounges currently offering expensive table service serving cigars champagne and liquor."*
>
> – ARIEL PAYOPAY, FOUNDER, LIERA CANNAGARS

### Leira Cannagars

With "flight times" of up to seven hours, this may just be one of the most expensive and luxurious flower products on the market. Available in classic cigar sizes including Cigarillo, Robusto, and Corona.

### Willie's Reserve

Willie's High Five Pack contains five whole-flower, no-trim, half-gram joints, Jarred flower offered in 1g, 2.5g, and ½ oz increments. Currently available in CO, WA, and CA.

Photo Courtesy: Erik Hecht

Photo Courtesy: Willie's Reserve

### Dope Pack

Dope Magazine works with producers and processors in each state to produce a branded pre-roll pack representing some of the finest quality cannabis in each state.

Photo Courtesy: Mark Coffin

### Illuminatus

Fine crafted "Red" Sativa and "Black" Indica pre-rolls from Illuminatus offers up elegantly designed pre-rolls that come in convenient five packs.

Photo Courtesy: Illuminatus

### Besito Minis

Whether you're looking to party, vibe, or chill, each mini-tin contains 10 hand-rolled mini joints for you to enjoy on your own, or with some socially distant friends. Available in Sour Diesel, Chemdawg, and Sundae Driver.

Photo Courtesy: Besito

*"Cannabis has evolved tremendously in the 30 years that I've been in the industry. The products, research, public sentiment, and regulations have all progressed. But the most impactful shift I've seen across all functions from cultivators to customers is more research and knowledge about the plant and its benefits. The information has empowered the industry and equipped us to make healthier, more effective, and more sustainable cannabis treatments based on science and it will continue to move cannabis forward because the facts are in our favor, cannabis is medicine."*

— DENNIS HUNTER, CO-FOUNDER CANNACRAFT, INC.

### Farmer And The Felon

Launched in March 2020, Farmer and the Felon serves as a platform for founders committed to social justice and equality in the canna-bis industry and our communities.

Photo Courtesy: Farmer and the Felon/CannaCraft

### House Of Cultivar

Understanding the importance of cannabis strain history, while remaining relevant in today's market is House of Cultivar's strength.

*"House of Cultivar is a collection of cannabis enthusiasts and cultivators. As such we are first and foremost attuned to the trends and cycle of strain popularity. As a farm, you are not just defined by how well you grow, but increasingly by WHAT you grow. This demand for the newest "hype" strains continues to grow, while at the same time their lifespan of relevancy continues to decrease. This has led us to start our own breeding program. House of Cultivar is uniquely qualified to honor the heirloom genetics of the past, and bridge that knowledge into the future."*

— JASON HUTTO, CEO AND FOUNDER, HOUSE OF CULTIVAR

Photo Courtesy: House of Cultivar

### Lowell Herb Co.

Lowell Herb Co. has elevated cannabis consumption with its sophisticated packaging and best-selling products. Based in California, the company's ethos is reflected through its bull logo that pays homage to the fight against cannabis prohibition.

Photo Courtesy: Lowell Herb Co.

### Toast

A high-end cannabis brand taking its cues from prohibition and the art deco and art nouveau styles of the time. Each Slice™ includes a hemp tube and specially designed filter that cleanses the smoke while leveling the burn.

> *"Toast has a simple mission to elevate cannabis. We start with a beautiful design backed by superior product integrity. We take cues from the hundreds of years of cannabis culture and then elevate it for the modern world."*
>
> - PUNIT SETH, CEO, TOAST

Photos Courtesy: Toast

### Weekenders

The modern approach to cannabis consumption, California-based Weekenders offers simple, blended pre-rolls offering lower THC and more functional effects without the unwanted consequences of highly concentrated THC products.

Photos Courtesy: Weekenders

### Sherbinskis
Created by Mario Guzman, cannabis tastemaker and curator of well-known cannabis genetics including Pink Panties, Sunset Sherbert, and the Gelato line—Bacio, Mochi, Acai berry, and Gello.

Photo Courtesy: Sherbinskis

### Pure Beauty
Launched in California's medical market, Pure Beauty was formed by Tracy Anderson, an integral part of the Marley Natural brand, and his two partners. Pure Beauty is a socially conscious fashion brand that creates quality cannabis products with a unique perspective.

Photo Courtesy: Pure Beauty/Nathanael Turner

*"We treat our community with respect by not dumbing anything down--we know that not everyone will like what we are doing and that is ok. Because the trade-off is, we have a community of people that love what we do and want to contribute and be part of it."*
- IMELDA WALAVALKAR, CO-FOUNDER, PURE BEAUTY

## Summary
Flower has traditionally been unbranded. Aromatic buds stored in glass vials identified by strain, rather than grower. But that is changing. Brands like Cookies, Dawg Star, Lowell Herb Co., Gold Leaf, House of Cultivar, Sherbinskis, Western Cultured, among others, are finding footholds among consumers. Much like the coffee bean market was once dominated by unbranded beans, but now heavily branded by individual coffee roasters. Will we see cannabis brands as prominent as coffee roasters like Starbucks? Not soon, but the trend seems inevitable—branding bud is well underway.[13]

# Access the industry's best market intelligence toolkit for free

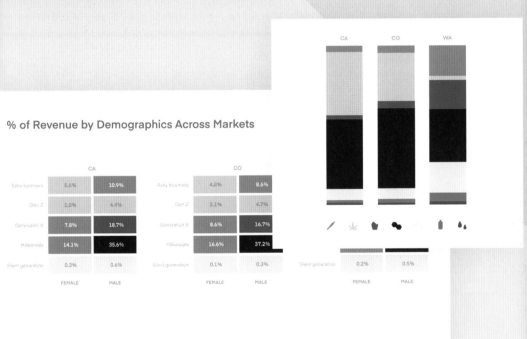

Test-drive the industry's leading cannabis dataset today. Sign up for Insights Pulse to explore our cannabis market read and get introductory access to our elite market intelligence tool kit.

**headset.io**

Photo Courtesy: Canndescent

# CANNABIS CONCENTRATES, OILS AND EXTRACTS

*"The leading trend in the cannabis industry is concentrate and extract production. Extractions using solvents such as butane and carbon dioxide, solvent-less methods such as ice-water extraction, dry-sifting, and hydraulic presses for rosin production, as well as advances in distillate technology all have revolutionized not only the consumption of concentrates themselves but also how edibles and topicals are produced. As cannabis becomes more legal, the glut of flowers grown will only contribute to more production of concentrates for many different purposes."*

— DANNY DANKO, FORMER SENIOR CULTIVATION EDITOR, HIGH TIMES MAGAZINE

## Cannabis Concentrates

Cannabis concentrates, also known as extracts, are significantly more potent than regular cannabis flower and their application as medicine have proven to be effective for patients suffering from all sorts of ailments. The extraction of cannabis concentrates is a complex and potentially dangerous process. Different types of cannabis extraction methods include:

- Non-hydrocarbons
- Dry Sieve
- Water
- $CO_2$
- Isopropyl Alcohol
- Hydrocarbons
- Butane / Propane
- Hexane

Mature cannabis flowers (buds) are coated with glands (trichomes) that contain medicinal compounds. Traditional cannabis consumption is characterized by the simple smoking of the dried and cured flowers coated with these glands containing the medicines. Extraction processes remove the trichomes from the vegetative matter of the leaf, leaving a concentrated wad, goo, hash, or powder of pure active medicinal compound.

Several alternative extraction methods have gained popularity in recent years-some intended for inhalation (butane, $CO_2$, propane, etc.) and others geared toward oral ingestion (ethanol, olive oil, coconut oil, etc.). It should come as no surprise that each substance reacts differently when used as a solvent, and the final product can be greatly affected by the process used to extract the highly coveted cannabis oil.

Photo Courtesy: CaliGold

The global cannabis market was worth just on $9 million in 2016 and will grow at a staggering 35% year on year for the next couple of years, to be worth an estimated $146 billion by 2025.[14] That's phenomenal growth, and yet inside of the industry is a sector growing even faster than that—the concentrate market.

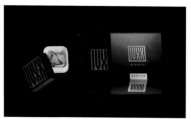

Photo Courtesy: IVXX

Grandview Research predicts that the oils segment of the market is expected to grow at over 40% per year for the next eight years. And historical facts validate this growth rate. In mature recreation-ally-recreationally-legal US States such as Colorado and Washington, extracts make up over 50% of the market. In a recent report by BDS Analytics,[15] they estimate the extracts market will grow from $2.9 billion in 2018 to a staggering $8.5 billion by 2022. By 2023, they estimate it will surpass flower sales.

---

*"I believe that the biggest trend that's beginning to shape the cannabis market is increased understanding of how this complex plant affects human physiology. We are seeing an increasing amount of cannabinoid products containing more than just THC come to market. Cannabinoid and terpene interactions are truly the future of cannabis therapies. Once we study these synergies further, we can maximize the benefits of this dynamic plant matrix to best treat certain conditions."*

- SARAH SANDOVAL, FOUNDER, JOLLYBEE

---

Photo Courtesy: Wick and Mortar/Jollybee

Cannabis concentrates have grown in popularity because of the wide variety of uses they have. Legally produced concentrates are sold for consumption in small lip-balm sized containers and are odorless when sealed. The market is booming more so, however, because cannabis concentrates are used to make edibles, topical ointments, capsules, and other packaged products that require professional-grade extraction.

*"Trending now more than ever are concentrates. People are seeking a cleaner alternative form of inhalation are finding the answer in concentrates. The lack of potential irritants inhaled during vaping or dabbing is far less than what you'd experience burning flower."*

- JUSE BARROS, EVERGREEN EXTRACTS

Courtesy: CaliGold

When purchased for consumption, they are named for the different consistencies created by the extraction. Known as waxes, oils, budders, and shatters, they are formulated for use in portable vaporizers and elaborate vaporizing 'rigs.' Vaporizers work similar to an electronic cigarette by heating the material to a temperature hot enough to convert it into an inhalable water vapor, which has only the briefest and faintest of odors and dissipates immediately in the air, unlike smoke. Vaporizers range in size from large at-home units to small, pen-sized devices that are used discreetly. Rigs, that look and work like bongs, require a blowtorch to heat the vaporizing element.[16]

*"We believe the growth of the concentrate market will continue as the cannabis industry evolves and consumers look toward new and innovative delivery methods that fit their lifestyles."*

– TOM ADAMS, BDS ANALYTICS

A closer look reveals there are many advantages of extracts over flower that are driving this growth boom, and it is not only about not smoking.

Courtesy: Lucid Oil

## Safety First

Oils, concentrates, extracts are generally considered safer than flower for two primary reasons. The first is the fact that people don't want to inhale carcinogenic smoke, which if consumed for a long period of time can be fatal. Oils and extracts are created under a combination of high temperature and high pressure in which the oil is purged of mold, mildew, and pesticides.[17]

## Consistent Cannabis

Oils are far more consistent and reliable than flower. Given the levels of automation and extraction technology that exist in the industry today, superior processing is creating consistency in dosing. Companies are now able to fine-tune components of the [cannabis] plant and create controlled combinations of compounds and terpenes.

### Abx Live

ABX Live resin captures the essence of the season's fresh harvest and delivers award-winning formulations for cannabis tastemakers seeking exclusive, true-to-flower cannabis experiences.

Photo Courtesy: AbsoluteXtracts/CannaCraft

### Rxo

An innovation in RSO products, RXO represents some of the highest quality and most accessible ethanol extracted cannabis oil on the market. Unlike traditional RSO, RXO can be smoked, dabbed, ingested, or applied topically.

Photo Courtesy: RXO/Chalice Farms

Photo Courtesy: Caliva

### Caliva

Caliva's Fresh Flower Vape cartridges are high potency and 100% cannabis, featuring single-source terpenes extracted directly from Caliva's own indoor-grown flower.

### Lowell Herb Co.

Lowell Herb Co.'s artisanal solventless live rosin is made with pure, cold-pressed cannabis oil and preserves the full cannabinoids and terpene profile from the raw plant. Available in jars, syringes, and vape cartridges.

Photo Courtesy: Lowell Herb Co.

"We're in a cannabis renaissance right now, fueled by legal, ethical brands passionate about creating best in class products. You can walk into any dispensary and discover a new product, strain, ratio, consumption method –the list is endless. What's really exciting is this wide assortment of products brought approachability to the cannabis space; we're seeing fun packaging more aligned with consumer packaged goods, low-dose ingestibles for the canna-curious, and a greater emphasis on product education, all of which aid with the de-stigmatization of the plant and industry as a whole. Especially in California, we have front row seats to so many new brands and products entering the market, each of which is tailored to suit a different type of consumer. It's gratifying to see the power of this plant being used to its full potential."

- MAGGIE CONNORS, CEO + FOUNDER, BESITO

Photo Courtesy: Besito

### Besito

Besito is a womxn-founded and queer-led, with a mission to be radically inclusive and make a space for women, BIPOC, and the LGBTQIA+ community within the industry.

### Solstice

Having collaborated with some of Washington State's best extraction artists for years, Solstice now builds their unique flavors and strains in their in-house lab. Their hydrocarbon extraction is done in small batches and represents a concentrated version of the award-winning varieties they offer in Flower and Pre-rolls.

Photo Courtesy: Solstice

Photo Courtesy: Western Cultured

### Western Cultured

Western Cultured is best known for its signature strains and quality flower, but they also offer some of the best concentrates in Washington State. Their flower strains are now available in vape cartridges via $CO_2$ extraction. SeaTown Lemon Haze's fruity flavor profile, along with its imaginative, uplifting effects, has made it one of their most popular oils. Other strains include our Perma Frost, Jurassic OGK, Island Lavender, and Cascade Connie.

### Sitka

Sitka produces a few different versions of hash. Lebanese Gold is a mix of Sativa strains. Lebanese Red is a mix of Indica strains. Cascade Cream is hash mixed with some $CO_2$ extract to add more of a punch. Sitka Lebanese Red Hashish has a deep mahogany color and is slightly oilier than their Lebanese Gold. Both are considered authentic hash for discerning connoisseurs.

Photo Courtesy: Sitka

## Polar Icetracts

Based in Washington state and partnered with Gold Leaf Gardens, this two-time award-winning processor of full melt bubble hash and rosin is the creator of Honey Diamonds and rosin infused Diamond Tip joints.

Photo Courtesy: Erik Hecht

Photo Courtesy: Circanna

## Nectar Craft

Nectar Craft's flagship line of terpene-rich $CO_2$ cartridges and oil applicators offer the same experience users have come to love from cannabis flower, without any of the hassle of remembering a lighter or smelling like smoke.

## Dosists

Science has proven that cannabis provides several functional benefits such as sleep aid, pain relief, euphoria, energy, and relaxation. To ensure safe and accurate dosing, Dosist developed the dose pen which uses superior vaporization elements built for activating the key cannabis compounds. The dose pen is available in two sizes—200 and 50 doses.

Photo Courtesy: Dosist

*"Much of the growth can be attributed to the beginner-friendly, brand identified vape cartridge subcategory."*

– Cannabis Business Times

## Willie's Reserve

Willie's Reserve™ pre-filled cartridges contain pure $CO_2$ cannabis distillate with cannabis-derived terpenes. That means no fillers, no cutting agents, or any other flavorings.

Photo Courtesy: Willie's Reserve

Photo Courtesy: Dawg Star

### Dawg Star

Dawg Star pre-filled cartridges contain pure $CO_2$ cannabis distillate with cannabis-derived terpenes. Available in Mind, Body, and Mood varieties.

### Lola Lola

Extracted from Grade A, organic cannabis. Small batch production formulated for superior aroma and flavor. No residual solvents or harmful additives. Batch tested for potency and consistency. First-generation, single-origin terpenes. Airtight glass storage maintains purity and freshness.

Photo Courtesy: Lola Lola

### Dopen

The Dopen™ vape pen and pre-filled cartridges contain pure $CO_2$ cannabis distillate with cannabis-derived terpenes. The Dopen is available in a variety of colors and limited-edition artist-series.

Photo Courtesy: Mark Coffin

### Elysium Fields

Elysium Fields Live Resin Cartridges are a 50:50 blend of Live Resin to Distillate. Thoughtfully crafted for the connoisseur looking for consistent quality and cost-effective Live Resin experience.

Photo Courtesy: Elysium Fields/Chalice Farms

### AbsoluteXtracts

From a deep understanding of the cannabis plant, terpenes, and robust cannabinoid profiles, AbsoluteXtracts formulations offer true-to-strain flavors and effects. ABX cartridges feature CCELL ceramic-coil technology.

Photo Courtesy: AbsoluteXtracts/CannaCraft

### Hellavated

Hellavated's oil cartridges are reasonably priced and come in "Strainz", Terpz" and "Profiles" varieties. Available in Washington, Oregon, and soon Oklahoma.

Photo Courtesy: Arbor Pacific/Hellavated

## Summary

The modern, legalized cannabis market is being redefined by product innovation. Technology is rapidly changing the face of consumer products in virtually every industry; and as more mainstream companies and investors flock to cannabis, they are bringing those technologies to the industry as well. Over the past few years arguably the most significant trend in cannabis has been the emergence of concentrates, extracts, and oils—especially, the vape category. Across 2018 and 2019, vape sales were the second-largest category following flower. Vape sales contributed 22 percent of revenues at dispensaries in Arizona, California, Colorado, and Oregon combined in 2018.[18]

apothecanna
**everyday**
body creme
cannabis infused bodycare
with natural and wildcrafted
plant ingredients to enhance
radiance and repair damage

mandarin
geranium
cedar
cannabis

8 fl oz ⊜ 236 ml

# CANNABIS TOPICALS

"When Apothecanna was created over 10 years ago, I had an idea that we could take this relatively misunderstood plant (cannabis) and present it in a more consumer-friendly format that people would have to stop and really think, 'is this an illicit drug, or is it functional, plant-based medicine?' Time has shown the latter to be true. The foundations that we set have held up in terms of color theory, product nomenclature, and form factors show through in cannabis product design today. It gives me a great deal of pride knowing that the standards we set a decade ago helped the consumer navigate this category and laid the foundation of cannabis as wellness."

— JAMES KENNEDY, FOUNDER, APOTHECANNA

## CANNABIS TOPICALS

Topicals are cannabis-infused lotions, balms, salts, and oils that are absorbed through the skin for localized relief of pain, soreness, and inflammation. Because they're non-psychoactive, topicals are often chosen by consumers who want the therapeutic benefits of cannabis without the cerebral euphoria associated with other delivery methods.

Strain-specific topicals attempt to harness certain terpenes and cannabinoids in a chemical profile in-line with whatever strains the processor wishes to imitate. Along with THC, CBD, THCA, and other cannabinoids, topical producers may also select ingredients and essential oils for additional relief, like cayenne, wintergreen, and clove, for example.

Cannabis-infused lotions, salves, oils, sprays, and other transdermal methods of relief work by binding to a network of receptors called CB2. These CB2 receptors are found throughout the body and are activated either by the body's naturally occurring endocannabinoids or by cannabis compounds known as "phytocannabinoids."[19]

Even if a topical contains active THC, it still won't induce that intense "high" you'd get from smoking or ingesting cannabis. With most topicals, cannabinoids can't breach the bloodstream; they only penetrate to the system of CB2 receptors. Transdermal patches, however, do deliver cannabinoids to the bloodstream and could have psychoactive effects with a high enough THC content.[20] [We'll look at transdermal patches in the "Innovative" section later].

Topicals are most popularly chosen for localized pain relief, muscle soreness, tension, and inflammation, but anecdotal evidence is beginning to show a widening spectrum of potential benefits, from psoriasis, dermatitis, and itching to headaches and cramping.

A THC-rich rub infused with cooling menthol and peppermint is a perfect way to wind down from a brutal workout or hike. For intense localized pain, you may try a warming balm that combines the deep painkilling properties of cannabinoids with a tingling, soothing sensation.

Different topicals have different benefits to offer depending on the way they are processed and the ingredients that are used, so experiment with various transdermal products to see what works for you. Medical marijuana states are seeing more and more options for topical remedies as time goes on, and for sufferers of pain and inflammation, it's worth exploring. You'd be surprised by the difference one ingredient makes.

### Cannabis Basics

Cannabis Basics utilize the goodness of organic hemp seed oil and adds premium cannabis whole-plant infusions and extractions, rich in multiple cannabinoids and terpenoids capturing the benefits of all 100+ cannabinoids.

> "Arthritic pain is caused by inflammation. Cannabis Basics products have [THCA] and CBD, both of which are anti-inflammatory. Active THC is not for inflammation, but when left in its acid form and combined with CBD, the two work to get rid of inflammation and the pain that comes with it."
>
> - AH WARNER, FOUNDER, CANNABIS BASICS

Photo Courtesy: Cannabis Basics

### Lord Jones

A name that paid homage to John Paul Jones, the Revolutionary War naval commander. A lesser-known fact is that he was fond of cannabis and grew hemp, as many of the colonists did. Lord Jones lab-tested topicals come in pure THC formulations, CBD formulations, as well as THC and CBD blends.

Photo Courtesy: Lord Jones

### Mary's Nutritonals

In addition to being the first to deliver transdermal cannabis products, Mary's was first-to-market the useful benefits of THCa and CBN, discovered harvesting techniques for the isolation of CBC, and continues to develop new cutting-edge approaches for isolating, manufacturing, and marketing medicinal cannabis.

Photo Courtesy: Mary's Nutritionals

### Dixie Brands

Synergy Relief CBD and THC balm is a powerful topical formula designed to penetrate the skin extremely fast. An effective blend of botanical extracts and cannabis in a fast penetrating gel base.

Photo Courtesy: Dixie Brands

### Care By Design

Rich in phytocannabinoids, flavonoids, and terpenes, Care By Design's CBD-rich cream provides soothing natural relief from aches and pains. Easily absorbs into skin without feeling greasy, sticky, or smelling like cannabis.

Photo Courtesy: Care By Design/CannaCraft

Photo Courtesy: Velvet Swing

### Velvet Swing

Velvet Swing is designed to relax blood vessels and ease muscle tension, leading to more enjoyable and pleasurable intercourse. It's the first 100% latex safe, water-soluble cannabis-infused lubricant free of parabens, glycerin and propylene glycol.

Photo Courtesy: Apothecanna

### Apothecanna

Apothecanna strives to create products with uncompromised purity, quality, and functionality. All products are formulated with active, natural, organic, and wildcrafted essential oils thoughtfully sourced from their native regions of the world.

### Cosmic View

Founded by a mother scientist and her cancer survivor daughter, Cosmic View's topicals and tinctures are made of only the purest organic cannabis, formulated with both science and traditional herbal wisdom in mind. Doctor formulated balms including "Deep Down", "Skin Salvation", "Viva La Vi" and "Cycle Sooth."

Photo Courtesy: Cosmic View / Maria Lokke

### Marley Natural

With outstanding moisturizing and non-greasy properties, cannabis Sativa oil is known for its health and skin beneficial qualities. Combined with Jamaican botanical ingredient blends such as lemongrass, ginger, and cerasee—sourced directly from the island—the Marley Natural Hemp Seed Body Care line offers formulas that promote and enhance your daily well-being.

Photo Courtesy: Marley Natural

## Summary

Terpenes and cannabinoids have merged with the mainstream via CBD. Born of scientific research, scientists are studying terpenes and other cannabinoids in hopes of developing new products. Cannabis enthusiasts leverage cannabis for everything from sleep to joint pain to anxiety relief. More than half of all cannabis consumers use it for what are essentially medical reasons.[21] And brands are meeting the demand with products like topicals, lotions, and even sex lube loaded with CBD and THC for pain and ... much more.

DÉFONCÉ
CHOCOLATIER

POPCORN

Dark bittersweet chocolate paired with half-popped
popcorn, pretzels, and kettle chips

MEDICAL CANNABIS

70%
CACAO

DÉFONCÉ
CHOCOLATIER

MINT

Malty milk chocolate studded with pe
and dark chocolate pieces

MEDICAL CANNA

180 MG        39
THC           CA

NET WT 3.5 c

DÉFO
CHOCOL

FONCÉ
COLATIER

DÉFO
CHOCOL

COF

Rich milk chocolate inter
Danish caramel waffles a

HAZELNUT

eet chocolate folded with caramelized cacao
hazelnuts, and toasted sweet baguette

Photos Courtesy: Defonce

# CANNABIS EDIBLES

"As a chef, access to unique ingredients enables creations that delight diners' palates. Cannabis consumers are demanding more complex products in both flavor and effects. Products that are poorly formulated or do not provide a pleasant experience for all of the senses are no longer being tolerated. Mobius marries unique and inspired ingredient sourcing, our palette, with creative formulations built for the evolving market palate."

– Bruce Milligan Founder, Mobius Beverage

## Cannabis Edibles

For as long as people have been enjoying cannabis as part of medical, spiritual, and recreational activities, it has been infused into food and drink. Edibles—the common name for cannabis-infused foods and sweets has been and will continue to be a popular consumption option for cannabis users.

The term cannabis-infused means that a cannabis product is used as an ingredient. THC, the active ingredient in cannabis is soluble in fat, meaning there's no loss of THC while cooking. This is why cannabis often is combined with butter and oils and then introduced into edibles.

Photos Courtesy: Dixie Brands

The candies and cookies found at recreational stores and dispensaries today have a direct predecessor that was sold in American stores in the 1800s. The Gunjah Wallah Company made a popular maple sugar hashish candy that they called a "most pleasurable and harmless stimulant" that was "guaranteed to be a complete mental and physical invigorator." Starting in 1864 and until about 1900, the candy was sold over the counter, advertised in newspapers, and even listed in the Sears-Roebuck catalog.[22]

> "Creating the best cuisine means using the best ingredients. The ability to separate, control, and reformulate the plants' terpenes and other key compounds so they can be used and consumed consistently is critical to the industry's evolution. I see a future where we will purchase each component of the plant separately to create our own 'recipes' for the flavor and fragrance profiles we desire."
>
> - JASON PINSKY, PRODUCER, BONG APPETIT, VICE MEDIA

Of course, with Prohibition, it was not until certain States began to legalize medical cannabis in the late 1990s that edible production picked up again. Patients' demand for high-quality edibles led to a variety of candies, sweets, lozenges, and other cannabis-infused, smoking alternatives.

Photos Courtesy: Botanica Seattle

## Edibles Provide A Safer Alternative To Smoking

Many patients believe that ingesting their cannabis is a healthier alternative to inhaling it because there is no exposure to carbon-rich smoke. Some patients, such as those on supplemental oxygen, turn to edibles when smoking is no longer an option. For patients with eating and digestive disorders, edibles are not only a great source of nausea-reducing CBD, but also a vital source of essential nutrients and calories. The same is true for cancer patients suffering from nausea caused by their treatments. A few patients choose edibles because they are a more discreet way to medicate, while others simply prefer the longevity of effects when ingesting cannabis compared to the fast-acting effects of smoking.

*"When you're going to try an edible, the packaging sets the tone for the experience you're going to have."*

*- Scott Palmer, Co-Founder, Kiva*

Because most edibles (except for alcohol tincture) are exposed to some kind of heat during the cooking process, many of the inactive cannabinoids such as THC-a and CBD-a, are converted to THC, CBD, and CBN. The cooking process, as well as the high levels of THC, found in edibles, work together to create the perfect treatment for many disorders, including chronic pain, muscle inflammation and spasms, auto-immune disorders, nervous system disorders, insomnia, and nausea—provided the patient is well enough to ingest the medication.

Photos Courtesy: Evergreen Herbal

## The Health Risks Associated With Consuming Edibles

Unfortunately, because there is no consistent system in place to oversee edible or infused product production, patients must exercise caution when purchasing edibles. Most states require nothing more than a commercial cooking license to sell to a dispensary. Laws are becoming more stringent in both medical and recreational states as expected.

Photos Courtesy: Dixie Brands

The quality of the cannabis that is used to infuse edibles is nearly impossible to determine. Some companies use edibles as a way to dispose of cannabis that otherwise couldn't be sold; like buds heavily laden with spider mites or mold. Because of this, edibles must be monitored and purchased from a trusted source.

Lawmakers and regulators in legal states throughout the country have mulled over infused edibles restrictions and warning labels in the face of reports of sharp increases in the number of children accidentally consuming cannabis products. While calls to Poison Control and hospital visits involving cannabis are far lower than similar numbers for other household products—like crayons, for example—they've nevertheless gone up significantly since legalization.[23]

To change that trend, States have adopted labeling requirements and set THC limits on edible products. Advocates of the labeling will dissuade children from consuming infused edibles that might otherwise appear to be normal, kid-friendly food. Let's take a look at current edible offerings below:

> "Since the first pot brownie was baked, the cannabis industry has avoided accountability and the scrutiny of modern food consumers. But as the industry matures, edible companies will have to answer to the sophisticated consumer who will question where ingredients come from and the labor standards behind them. This is a good thing and it will push the industry forward to new levels of quality and transparency."
> - MIKE APPEZZATO, CO-FOUNDER, GOOD COOP

Photos Courtesy: Evergreen Herbal

"*Cannabis is becoming a CPG [Consumer Product Good] like Gatorade® and But-terfinger®, with one very distinct advantage, the consumer is getting stoned! This means it's almost impossible for the consumer not to have a positive experience. The brands that will distinguish themselves are the ones that understand the experience, and the interaction begins before consumption of their product. The relationship starts before the consumer interacts with the product.*"

- Marco Hoffman, Founder, Evergreen Herbal

## Kiva

Colorado-based Dixie Brands is perhaps one of the powerhouse brands manufacturing edibles, candy, and beverages. Their chocolate truffles are an exquisite delectable that packs a punch.

Photo Courtesy: KIVA

"*As more states are beginning to allow the growth of both medical and adult-use markets, brands have to be more strategic in marketing individual products to multiple audiences that are looking for very different things.*"

- Steve Miller, Director of Marketing, KIVA

Photo Courtesy: Beboe

## Beboe

Beboe was created for those looking for a mindful and elevated cannabis experience. A slightly herbaceous, bursting blueberry flavor loaded with 10mg of CBD per mint and 3mg of THC from cold water processed Indica-blend hash.

### AbsoluteXtracts

ABX gummies combine all-natural ingredients and premium cannabis oil to bring you three delicious, small-batch gummy flavors. These gluten and gelatin-free, vegan gummies are crafted by culinary expert, Chef Matt Kulczycki.

Photo Courtesy: AbsoluteXtracts/CannaCraft

### Ruby Sugar

Ruby cannabis-infused sugar was created to easily incorporate into one's everyday food and drink. Only 15 calories, vegan, fat-free, gluten-free, non-GMO, and no additives. Portable, discreet and tastes great.

Photos Courtesy: Deep Cell

### Lord Jones

A name that paid homage to John Paul Jones, the Revolutionary War naval commander. A lesser-known fact is that he was fond of cannabis and grew hemp, as many of the colonists did. Lord Jones lab-tested edibles come in pure THC formulations, CBD formulations, and THC and CBD blends. They pride themselves on being a low-dose company, offering only 5, 10, and 20 mg options.

Photo Courtesy: Lord Jones

### Leafs By Snoop

Dogg Treats from Leafs By Snoop are individually hand-poured and pulled using natural extract and premium cannabis oil. Each package of Fruit Chews Dogg Treats contains 10 chews, and each one contains 10 mg of active THC.

Photos Courtesy: Leafs By Snoop

### Willie's Reserve

When Annie Nelson first made chocolates to keep her husband company on the road, she had no idea they would become a storied part of Willie's famous stash. Willie's Reserve™ now offers these legendary, all organic, gluten-free, vegetarian chocolates available to all. Annie's original whole flower recipe infuses each piece of chocolate with 5mg of THC, perfect for those new to cannabis.

Photo Courtesy: Willie's Reserve

Photo Courtesy: The Good Ship

### The Good Ship

The Good Ship Company is a Seattle based maker of premium cannabis-infused baked goods, chocolates, and confections.

### Dixie

Dixie offers up its infused vitalizing, awakening and relaxing mints from Dixie provides a low, consistent dosage and fits discreetly into your pocket. They're formulated with premium ingredients to enhance your alertness, increase your stamina or provide you with a soothing and relaxing effect.

Photo Courtesy: Dixie Brands

### Willie's Reserve

Annie's Infused Chocolates are handcrafted, infused chocolates made from carefully sourced ingredients. A "Zero Crap Policy" is followed in Annie's kitchen, which results in fair trade, antioxidant-rich chocolates that are gluten-free, vegan, and 100% raw.

Photo Courtesy: Willie's Reserve

### Willie's Reserve

The all-new lineup of infused edibles from Willie's Reserve™ sings Willie Nelson's commitment to good times and good practices. Available in the following flavors: Cherry Watermelon, Fresh Maple Blossom, Honeysuckle Hot, Northwest Berry, Peppermint, Sour Tangie, and Strawberry Lemonade.

Photo Courtesy: Willie's Reserve

### Spot

Simply designed, SPOT is crafted in Seattle, Washington. Following their motto, "precise, consistent, delicious."—each package clearly shows the cannabis experience and potency of the product.

Photo Courtesy: Botanica Seattle

Photo Courtesy: Botanica Seattle

### Mr. Moxie's Mints

Created by Botanica Seattle, Mr. Moxey's Mints have been the leading mint brand in Washington for over 12 months. Now available in other states, this particular brand has been at the forefront of the micro-dosing trend. Available in a variety of flavors, Mr. Moxey's Mints contain 5mg of THC per mint.

### Chalice Farms

Chalice's nutritionally enhanced and award-winning fruit chew line has established itself as a trusted and premium brand for health and wellness, as well as for recreational enjoyment. Vegan, Gluten-Free, Soy Free, Made with Real Fruit Puree, Beet Sugar, Sunflower Lecithin and MCT Coconut Oil.

Photo Courtesy: Chalice Farms

## Caligold

For every product purchased, CALIGOLD donates at least one percent to its nonprofit Casa del Alma, fostering the preservation of Colombia's indigenous Nasa Yuwe cultural heritage and language through education and sustainable farming.

Photo Courtesy: Caligold

Photo Courtesy: Defonce

## Defonce

Défoncé was founded in 2015 by Apple alum Eric Eslao. Drawing on the iconic brand as inspiration to create the world's best cannabis-infused chocolate, Eslao leads a dynamic team of creatives and food-manufacturing veterans, elevating taste and design in cannabis edibles.

## Supreme Organics

Cultivated, extracted, and crafted in their state-of-the-art downtown Los Angeles kitchen, supreme organics offers a variety of edibles including hard candy, fruit gummies, fruit chews, almond butter/peanut butter/caramel cups, peppermint patties, dark chocolate, caramel, almond, nougat bars, dark chocolate, caramel, almond, nougat bar minis, among others.

Photo Courtesy: Supreme Organics

Photo Courtesy: Ruby Sugar

## Ruby Salted Caramel

Innovators of cannabis-infused cane sugar and Himalayan salt, Ruby is now moving into other edibles such as salted caramels.

## Hot Sugar

Hot Sugar also comes in a variety of flavors, including plain, citrus, warm marshmallow, creamy caramel, chocolate, Pomtini, and Blue Raspberry Weed Rita. One serving of Hot Sugar contains 10 mg of powdered THC and can be purchased where the Phat Panda brand is sold.

Photo Courtesy: Phat Panda

### Kiva

The name Camino was inspired by the historic El Camino Real, the 600-mile California road that connects some of the most beautiful and inspiring landscapes in the state. Each flavor of Camino was designed to transport you to a specific location and put you in a "California State of Mind."

Photo Courtesy: Kiva

### Lowell Herb Co.

These micro-dose mints are the perfect way to enjoy Lowell any time, day or night. Made with the highest quality all-natural ingredients these peppermint mints are sure to delight. Sold in 40-2.5mg mints per tin.

Photo Courtesy: Lowell Herb Co.

### Satori

Satori's handcrafted cannabis confections are made from gourmet ingredients, including premium chocolate infused with precise doses of pure cannabis oil over whole fruits and nuts.

Photo Courtesy: Satori/CannaCraft

## Deli

Caliva is entering the edible category with the launch of its DELI Nickels Gummy Rounds, a new line of THC infused gummies under its sub-brand DELI, known for providing Delicious, Delightful, and Deliberately affordable cannabis options. Available in Sour Green Apple, Mixed Berry, Passionfruit, Mango.

Photo Courtesy: Deli/Caliva

## Hellavated

Hellavated's power-packed infused "Gummiez" contains 10mg per piece (100 mg per pouch) and comes in a variety of flavors including Mango Dragon, Water Yer Melon, Strawberry Haze and Razberry Blitz.

Photo Courtesy: Arbor Pacific/Hellavated

# Summary

Gummies are the most popular form of edible cannabis on the market. In California alone, they represent 27 percent of all edible products, dwarfing things like chocolate bars (7 percent) and baked goods (10 percent). The most popular flavor in the state? Watermelon, followed by blackberry, lemon, blue raspberry, cherry cola, sour apple, and strawberry.[24]

As the micro-dosing movement gains footholds across the country, the standard dose is shrinking. In California so far this year, for example, the top six chocolate bar products are all divided into 20 servings, with each serving containing five milligrams of THC. It has taken a lot of small steps over a long period of time, but micro-dosing is beginning to change how we think about cannabis edibles servings.

With CBD products lining the shelves of traditional stores across the nation, we also see a rise in CBD-rich products within the medicinal and adult-use cannabis market(s). This is true across form factors including a rise in sales of CBD-rich tincture as well as CBD-rich chocolate. In fact, while CBD-rich chocolate SKUs grew 242 percent, overall cannabis-infused chocolate sales dropped by 14 percent in Colorado. At the close of 2018, CBD-rich chocolate accounted for 61 percent.[25]

BLAZE
CANNABIS INFUSED SODA
Orange Cream Pie
100MG THC
CONTAINS NO FRUIT JUICE
6.3 FL OZ (187 ML)
PURE CANE SUGAR

# CANNABIS BEVERAGES

*"Micro-dosing will help the beverage category reach its full potential. Beverages are only social if you can have a number of them in one sitting. Drinking all the alcohol you are planning on drinking in the first 10 minutes of stepping into a bar makes no sense. Micro-dosed beverages, like CANN, mimic the strength of a light beer or glass of wine and have the ability to convert mainstream consumers to cannabis drinkers."*
- JAKE BULLOCK, CO-FOUNDER AND CEO, CANN

There really is no difference between the effects of oral dosing with cannabis, whether in an edible or drinkable form. With edibles, as with infused beverages, THC becomes 11-Hydroxy-THC after passing through the stomach and liver; rather than delta-9-THC entering into the bloodstream which happens while smoking.[26]

The beverage category is unique in that cannabis-infused beverages allow for several things that other form factors don't:

- Infused liquids are easily and discreetly consumed.
- They typically contain fewer calories per serving than a sweet dessert edible.
- They often can be used as a replacement for an alcoholic beverage.
- They are often served in powder form, allowing for ease of transport and convenience.

Here is just a sampling of the burgeoning cannabis-infused beverage offerings:

## Coffee And Tea

It's been proven that there is higher solubility of THC in a hot beverage than with a cold one. Several companies, including the original Jane's Brew, offer teas, coffees, cappuccinos, and mochas in a K-Cup format for an instant, discreet medication. Various dosages and decaf options are available, as well as infused creamers.

## Soda And Juice

Thanks to new extraction and infusion technologies developed in legal markets, companies are finding new ways to create deliciously sweet carbonated beverages infused with cannabis oil. Citrus-flavored Sprig soda, out of southern California, packs a punch with 45mg of THC per can, with absolutely no cannabis taste. Evergreen Herbal based in Washington manufactures a soda line including infused versions of cola, cherry cola, root beer, ginger beer, and orange. Other manufacturers and processors include CANN, Craft Elixirs, Dixie Brands, Mobius Beverages, mood33, Tarukino manufacturers of Happy Apple, Mirth Provisions, among others.

## Cocktails, Mixers And Syrup

Concocted from everything including exotic fruits and herbs to grandma's old recipe, cannabis-infused syrups are quite popular. Mixed with a carbonated soda, juice, hot tea, or any other refreshing and/or calming beverage.

*"Not every state is keen to let people mix cannabis and alcohol in the same setting, but in Washington State's recreational market, it's fast becoming a trend. Craft Elixirs is just one company combining herbology with cannabis-infused simple syrups."*

-JAMIE HOFFMAN, FOUNDER, CRAFT ELIXIRS

### *Hi-Fi Hops*

Expertly crafted, cannabis-infused, sparkling hoppy water from Lagunitas is made from the finest hops in the Yakima Valley. Lagunitas has partnered with AbsoluteXtracts who infuses the water with a proprietary cannabis emulsion, ensuring consistency in potency, flavor, and effects.

Photo Courtesy: Lagunitas/CannaCraft

### Mobius

Restorative raspberry paired with the perfect scientific ratio of CBD is what you'll get when you drink a Möbius beverage, providing you with a welcome regime for supporting your body's harmony and balance.

Photo Courtesy: Mobius Beverages

Photo Courtesy: Lahua USA

### Olala

Born in Hawaii. Raised in Washington. Olala cannabis-infused sodas, sparkling waters, terpene tonics are crisp, light, and refreshingly sweet. Winner of three Dope Cup Awards, Olala beverages are available in a variety of flavors including Spiced CranApple, Blue Raspberry, Honeydew Melon, Orange Cream, Pineapple, Fruit Punch, Classic Cola, and Lemon Lime Citrus.

*"The leading trend that I've seen as pervasive in the industry is to build a luxury brand. When you think about it though, it's kind of an oxymoron as the general public doesn't see cannabis as a luxury product, but many producers and processors want to be perceived as producing and/or processing best of breed. To build a reputation in this early market, products must be built on quality. Companies have to make delightful products to help the industry grow out of its current state."*

— NOEL REMIGIO, CO-FOUNDER, OLALA BRANDS

### Happy Apple

Happy Apple cannabis-infused sparkling apple beverage; reminiscent of a cider but without alcohol, Happy Apple isn't just another sugar-laden cannabis drink; it's fresh and crisp and made for joyful sipping.

Photo Courtesy: SORSE Technology

### Blaze

Blaze cannabis-infused soda made with distillate, pure cane sugar, and lots of love. Available in a variety of flavor favorites including Ginger Beer, Cherry Cola, Root Beer, Cola, Orange Cream, Grape, Wild Mountain Honey, and traditional Lemon Lime—in varying doses for beginner, novice, and experts alike.

Photo Courtesy: Evergreen Herbal

### Legal

A perfect example of a prohibition brand archetype,
Legal is a refreshing concoction made from all-natural
ingredients. Choose from Pomegranate Power, Lemon
Ginger Dream, and Rainier Cherry.

Photo Courtesy: Mirth Provisions

> *"Beverages could be an important entryway into the cannabis market for many first-
> time users who might not know how to roll a joint and want to ease into the drug
> slowly. It's much more approachable than many of the past and current stigmas."*
>
> — ADAM STITES, MIRTH PROVISIONS FOUNDER

### Dixie Elixirs

Dixie Elixirs come with a child-resistant dosing cap allowing patients to
find their perfect dose. Elixirs are made with pure cane sugar and have
no artificial coloring or flavors. Homogenization technology increases
bioavailability and reduces uptake time.

Photo Courtesy: Dixie

### Hi Lite

Satisfy your thirst with this organic fruit cannabis-infused beverage, sweetened with organic cane sugar. Includes a see-through milligram indicator that allows for accurate dosing. Vegan, no gluten, non-GMO, no artificial sweeteners—and comes with a child-resistant cap.

Photo Courtesy: Evergreen Herbal

---

*"The one trend that has created the passion in me to pioneer THC and CBD infused beverages is actually not something every entrepreneur gets into this industry thinking about, but to me was the greatest inspiration. The global awakening to the power of Plant Medicines, which includes everything from cannabis to psychedelic mushrooms to ayahuasca, has shown me the incredible healing power, physically, mentally, and spiritually that the plant kingdom can offer us. I believe cannabis is the gateway herb, not the gateway drug it was demonized to be."*

- ERIC SCHNELL, MOOD33 CO-FOUNDER AND CEO

---

### Mood33

Inspired by ancient herbal remedies, Ayurveda principles, and traditional Chinese herbal medicine, mood33 infusions were developed by organic beverage pioneers and life-long cannabis advocates to celebrate the plant's mood-enhancing health benefits and wellness-inducing qualities.

Photo Courtesy: mood33

### Cann

Launched in 2019, Cann is the first cannabis-infused social tonic that's quickly grown into California's #1 lowest dose cannabis beverage. Cann's an approachable and shareable product comes in three flavor profiles including Blood Orange Cardamom, Lemon Lavender, and Grapefruit Rosemary.

Photo Courtesy: CANN

### Vertus

Vertus is an alcohol-free, champagne-style beverage born in Washington state. Vertus is free of the unpleasant weed taste and smell. Instead, you experience a slightly sweet, slightly dry, effervescent mouthful.

Photo Courtesy: SORSE Technology

### Reeb

SORSE Technology brings us Reeb—beer spelled backward—the first THC infused non-alcoholic brew in Washington state. Available in bitter barley commonly referred to as Pale Ale and light barley commonly known as Pilsner.

Photo Courtesy: SORSE Technology

### Pearl

Pearl is a revolutionary cannabis-infused food and beverage mixer. With Pearl, you can infuse your favorite drinks and food without the taste or smell of cannabis. Concentrated and easy to use, Pearl, contains zero calories, zero fat, zero cholesterol, zero sugar.

Photo Courtesy: SORSE Technology

## Summary

The Beverage market is certainly one to watch, especially as the market develops. It's an interesting category because it's small. At less than 2% of the total market in most states, there's lots of room for growth. And it's growth, as evidenced by those 0.5% or higher leaps in market share. The Beverage market seems to be most established in Washington State, with the largest overall market share. However, Colorado has a solid segment diversity, which suggests that consumers are open to Beverages.

The Beverages market, while not massive, presents several unique insights about the state of the cannabis industry overall. First and foremost, it shows us how the piecemeal, state-by-state pattern of legalization affects sales. Even among states that legalized at the same time, like Colorado and Washington, price and consumer preferences vary wildly, as evidenced by our data on flavors.

Had cannabis been legalized at a federal level, we could expect to see a lot more consistency across the country, as brands would be nationwide, not limited to individual states. While many brands do cross state lines, the first-to-market brands in each state will shape the market, as Legal did in Washington.

That said, there are still some overarching trends to the category. Sodas aren't just popular in Washington, enjoying a healthy share of the market in other states as well. They're also growing that share, with only Mocktails joining them as a growing segment. Drops, Mixes, Elixirs and Syrups have been significant players in the Beverage market in the past but increased interest in Beverages as a discrete packaged consumable, ala six-packs of beer or 20oz sodas, could shift the market away from that segment.

Indeed, the trends that do stand out in the Beverages market point to this becoming even more of a thing. Especially in dosage. The average cannabis consumer doesn't have enough tolerance to imbibe an entire 100mg Beverage in one sitting, so a lot of those were probably divisible into smaller doses, via a dropper or attached cup. The rise in low dose products suggests that single-serve products are gaining in popularity—CANN is a perfect example. It's premature to say that 5mg THC sodas will become ubiquitous, but the theory that non-drinkers turning to cannabis beverages as an alternative isn't entirely untenable.

Beverages won't singlehandedly transform how cannabis is consumed, but trends within the Beverage category can tell us a lot about shifting consumer interest. While certainly a category to watch, which direction it takes—either towards a single-serve, mass-market consumable or back towards a specialty cannabis product—has a lot to say about more general consumer preferences in and for cannabis.

Photo Courtesy: Cosmic View / Maria Lokke

# CANNABIS TINCTURES AND CAPSULES

## What Are Tinctures?

Perhaps one of the oldest means of consuming cannabis, tinctures offer ease of use, convenience, and higher bioavailability than other means of uptake. By definition, a tincture is an herbal solution made with alcohol as the primary extraction solvent. In the cannabis product realm, the term tincture is used to define concentrated liquid preparations that are meant to be applied topically or orally. Tinctures are versatile and allow for accurate dosing and titration.[27]

The cannabis tincture and capsule market is overflowing with a wide variety of brand offerings; perhaps, because it's easier to produce tinctures and capsules than beverages, edibles and/or other form factors. The following is a brief overview of some of the leading tincture and capsule makers in the market:

### The Root Of It All

TROIA essential oil is infused with an Ayurvedic blend of lemongrass, bergamot, and ylang-ylang – ingredients known to calm restlessness and promote comfort, tranquility, stress relief, and a quiet mind. All TROIA tinctures are plant-based, gluten-free, vegan, and allergy-friendly.

Cannabis tinctures can be made from the raw cannabinoids THCA and CBDA or can be heated (a process known as decarboxylation) to convert the raw cannabinoids to THC and CBD. Most preparations are labeled with the main cannabinoids.

Tincture, by definition, is made with alcohol as the solvent. With cannabis however, you can also find tinctures made with MCT oil, glycerin, and even olive oil (these are all technically elixirs). While there is some debate in the cannabis universe about which type of tincture is best, you can't go wrong with olive oil for better shelf life and a healthier option.

Photo Courtesy: The Root Of It All

## How Do Tinctures Work?

When applied sublingually, tinctures are absorbed through the body via blood vessels located under the tongue. This allows for relatively fast delivery directly into the bloodstream, where the cannabinoids can then be distributed to the cannabinoid receptors throughout the brain and body. Sublingual absorption provides onset as quickly as 15 minutes. Cannabinoids not absorbed under the tongue will travel with the carrier liquid through the digestive tract, where they're absorbed like an edible; so, tinctures can present delayed onset of effects as well. When blended with food or drink, tinctures act in much the same way as edibles.[28]

Photo Courtesy: Dixie Brands

## Dosing Details

The appropriate dose of a tincture depends on a variety of factors, including a person's individual endocannabinoid makeup and the desired effects they wish to receive. In tincture applications, a method called "self-titration" is recommended to determine your optimal dosage. Titration essentially means working up to the desired effect, starting with a low dose and adding gradually until the desired effect is reached.

## What Are Cannabis Capsules?

A pill-sized, dissolvable cylinder is used as a vehicle to administer medication through ingestion. Capsule shells, of which there are many variants, can contain any form of cannabis, even decarboxylated flower. Capsules range from single cannabinoid to full-spectrum or strain-specific oil, providing consumers with a myriad of choices to suit their exact needs. These often function as safer alternatives to combusting or vaping bud.[29]

## What Are Capsules And Why Are They Preferred By Some Users?

Patients often opt for capsules instead of combustible flower or vaporizable products because capsules offer an easier and more convenient method of ingesting the medication. Capsules also provide patients with exact dosing information, which allows them to plan for consistent effects. Typically, capsules containing cannabis are not cultivar—or strain-specific and are labeled per their cannabinoid contents, e.g. THC and CBD capsules.

### Papa & Barkley

All Papa & Barkley products start with clean cannabis and supporting ingredients; and are crafted using a proprietary lipid process that infuses the whole cannabis plant profile into the end products without introducing chemical solvents or employing harsh extraction methods. This whole plant process, while labor-intensive, allows Papa & Barkley to keep the plant and all its beneficial compounds intact.

Photo Courtesy: Papa & Barkley

### Dixie Synergy Tablets

Synergy tablets were developed to maximize the effect of a low dose, discrete and convenient delivery tablet. An excellent option for those wanting the extended calming and inflammatory benefits from a high CBD-ratio edible without all the associated calories and sugar. Sold in child-resistant secure packaging. Nut-free, gluten-free.

Photo Courtesy: Dixie Brands

*"Trust is the only true basis for brand love; and as marketers, that is our ultimate goal. The industry and category are growing, and our audience is evolving from 'weed smokers' to 'cannabis consumers' – fueled by an increasingly large 'canna-curious' audience. Acting as 'partner and guide' to our multitude of stakeholders including consumers, retailers, budtenders, legislators, and other interest groups, is key."*

— ANDREW FLOOR, VP MARKETING, DIXIE BRANDS

### Care By Design

Care By Design created the standard in personalized care within cannabis by being first to market with 5 ratio blends of CBD and THC. All products are made with cannabis oil extracted from sun-grown, whole-plant, high-CBD strains without the use of toxic chemicals.

Photo Courtesy: Care By Design/CannaCraft

### Elysium Fields

Elysium Fields tinctures are geared toward the seasoned cannabis user, looking for a more potent and more strain-specific sublingual alternative. Exquisitely crafted, high potency distillate combined with strain-specific Live Resin creates a high potency and true-to-the-plant experience.

Photo Courtesy: Elysium Fields/Chalice Farms

Photo Courtesy: Cosmic View / Maria Lokke

### Cosmic View

Cosmic View's CBD-rich tinctures are made with locally made, cold-pressed Tuscan blend olive oil, and the finest high-CBD whole plant crude $CO_2$ extracted sun-grown cannabis to create a refined flavor profile with maximum health benefits.

## How Do Capsules Work?

Immediate-release capsules work identically to edibles. They enter the body through the mouth and are absorbed through the stomach. The absorbed compounds are then metabolized in the liver. This is where THC is metabolized into a compound called 11-hydroxy-THC, which is more potent than THC, has a longer half-life (which refers to the drug's elimination from the bloodstream), and can have more of a sedative effect than THC alone. The liver's metabolizing mechanism is unique to each individual, which is why edibles and capsules can convey different effects for different people. This entire process can take between 45 to 180 minutes or up to 3 hours.[30]

Timed-release capsules follow the identical path of digestion, but the delivery of their contents can be delayed or drawn out over a period of time depending upon the capsule shell's constituent ingredients. Those engineered with liposomes and drug-polymer conjugates, such as hydrogels, allow for the timed release of their contents. Timed-release capsules use these protective and inert ingredients to neutralize stomach acid for slower methods of release.

As a rule of thumb, the cannabis genus contains two types of plants: hemp plants and cannabinoid-rich plants commonly called marijuana. Hemp, which lacks robust terpenoid and cannabinoid spectrums, is grown for fiber and seed oil while cannabinoid-rich plants are grown for their full range of cannabinoids (THC, CBD, THCA, etc.) and other medicinally beneficial compounds. Both industrial hemp and marijuana are used in cannabis capsules but harvesting industrially grown hemp as a source of CBD is far from optimal.[31]

### Cookies

Cannabis oil in an easy to consume, precisely dosed gel cap. Ideal for long-lasting relief. Cookies add high-quality organic coconut oil (MCT) to aid absorption of the cannabis oil for optimal benefits. Precisely dosed amount of THC. Long-lasting, easy to consume, odorless, and flavor-free gel capsule.

Photo Courtesy: Cookies

### AbsoluteXtracts

CBD-rich soft gels are easy-to-swallow, and each is laboratory tested to verify CBD and THC content for precise and consistent dosing. Slow-release time and ideal for long-term relief.

Photo Courtesy: AbsoluteXtracts/CannaCraft

## Summary

Because capsules provide reliable and consistent dosing, they may be an ideal fit for those patients suffering from chronic pain, cancer, or HIV. A capsule is a safe way to ingest cannabis that doesn't involve smoking or vaping. As such, it represents a feasible choice for older patients, children, and people with respiratory issues. The lack of smoke and the ability of a patient to ingest a capsule anywhere, anytime makes it an even more discreet option than vaping and tinctures.

And because capsules contain no unnecessary calories or ingredients, patients reap all of the holistic benefits of the medicine without having to be concerned about added sugar and fat commonly used in cannabis edibles. They are also a great choice for patients who are new to cannabis, have never used tinctures or vaporizers before, and simply feel more comfortable using a medication form that they're already familiar with.

Capsules are a reliable and consistent form of administration that's ideal for patients seeking medical cannabis that can be taken discreetly; doesn't introduce harmful smoke or unnecessary ingredients into the body and takes the guesswork out of dosing. As with all forms of cannabis administration, you should research your options and inform your healthcare provider if you believe capsules are the best option for your particular circumstances.[32]

# 100% THC™
# 0% WTF

# INNOVATIVE CANNABIS PRODUCTS

> *"As consumer tastes change, there is a clear trend toward refined product form factors. Standard consumption methods like smoking, vaping and ingesting, don't provide specific reliable experiences. Inhaling a drug is out of vogue for many people and edibles are too slow and unpredictable for most situations. Refined infused products like sublingual strips and transdermal patches promise to fix these underlying issues and provide consumers with the experience(s) they're seeking."*
>
> - JOSH KIRBY, CO-FOUNDER, KINSLIPS

Today's new legal cannabis form factors are quite innovative and range from sublingual slips and sprays to transdermal patches.

## Understanding Bioavailability And Dosing

Research shows that transdermal delivery is the most effective method of delivering cannabis to the body as it enters the bloodstream directly. When smoked or eaten, patients may lose up to 70 percent of the cannabis consumed via air vaporization, metabolism, and stomach acid, which is inefficient and makes accurate dosing difficult. Transdermal products are so effective that the dosing of a standard 10mg patch may be equivalent to that of an 80mg edible.

## Transdermal Patches And Pens

Transdermal drug delivery—a route of administration wherein active ingredients are delivered across the skin for systemic distribution—has the potential to directly heal a specific injured area of the body. The patch provides a controlled release of the medication, either through using a porous membrane to let the medication be absorbed gradually by the skin or through embedding thin layers of the medicine in the adhesive that melt from the consumer's body heat.

### Papa & Barkley

This slow-release patch sticks to the skin, offering pain relief through transdermal delivery of full-spectrum cannabinoids. With a quick and easy single application, you get up to 12 hours of relief for your whole body.

*Photos Courtesy: Papa & Barkley*

### Mary's Medicinals - Transdermal Pen

Designed as an accompaniment to our patches, Mary's transdermal gel pens are the perfect resource for patients managing breakthrough pain or for creating blended cannabinoid ratios. The light gel is placed directly on the skin and gently rubbed in for rapid relief.

*Photo Courtesy: Mary's Medicinals*

---

*"Right now, the exciting catalyst in the cannabis industry is the space opened by recreational legislation for scientific discovery and lab testing. Where only a couple of years ago labs that would test cannabis were shady and too expensive for a lot of startups, now there are professional labs readily available in almost every medical and recreational state. With the ability to step away from the conjecture of cannabis past and step into the light of actual scientific fact, the industry is adapting to fit into scientific realms. We have adapted our marketing techniques to fit into this hard-facts culture that testing and analytics are awakening in the business."*

— CELESTE MIRANDA, THE CANNABIS MARKETING LABS

---

### Flyright - Transdermal Patch

Like all medicines, an individual's dosage is based on many factors such as age, body composition, diagnosis, etc. One patch is a typical dose for most patients, although some prefer to cut a patch into halves or even quarters, while others may use more than one patch to attain relief.

*Photo Courtesy: Flyright/Mobius*

### The Benefits Of Sublingual Administration

The major advantage of the sublingual administration method is that the THC and/or CBD is rapidly absorbed through the sublingual artery, your body's main blood supply to your tongue. This artery arises from the external carotid artery, which, in turn, is close to the internal carotid artery. This allows the medicine to quickly reach your brain.

Further, the THC and/or CBD doesn't come in contact with the acids in your stomach like other edibles do. That fact alone serves to keep many of the beneficial chemicals in your cannabis sublingual more complete and readily available for use in your body.

Sublingual absorption effectively removes a step—digestion—that can have slight but destructive consequences to the chemical makeup of the cannabis you put into your body.[33]

### Kinslips Sublingual Slips

Kin Slips are compact, portable, and dissolve under your tongue delivering a precise dose quickly. Their carefully crafted blends of cannabinoids, terpenes, and natural ingredients are formulated for positive effects on lifestyle and health. 100% natural and plant-based with an overall great taste.

Photos Courtesy: Kinslips/Kandid Kush Studios

### Dixie Lift

Drift™, a fast-acting sublingual spray that offers the ease of a vape pen without the smoke. Take it along to bars, concerts, parties, and anywhere else you want to pass the joy around. Each bottle contains 100 mg of THC from the best locally sourced cannabis, infused into organic, cold-extracted peppermint oil.

Photos Courtesy: Dixie Brands

*"The leading trend in the cannabis industry today is the emergence of micro-dosing. While higher doses have a great place for treating more severe medical conditions like chronic pain, sub-threshold doses are becoming used for more nuanced situations since they can be consumed without the individual being overwhelmed with the psychoactive effects of a strong dose. Micro-dosing lets consumers gain the benefits of THC while avoiding the potential negative side effects that can come from psychoactivity like anxiety, which ultimately opens the door for alleviating a much wider variety of ailments."*

- Shanel Lindsay, Founder and President, Ardent

## Summary

Newer product categories are emerging. The new breeds of products include dissolvable powders that can be added to food or beverages, inhalers, orally dissolvable strips, sex lube, and even suppositories. While sales of these emerging product categories remain relatively small, with added awareness and trialing, their market share will soon grow.

## CONCLUSION

When Colorado kicked-off legal adult-use cannabis sales in the United States in 2014, unbranded flower fully dominated the marketplace, capturing more than 60 percent of all sales. Concentrates, edibles, and topicals were far behind.[34]

Five years later, multiple states enjoy legalized recreational cannabis sales, including the largest cannabis economy in the world, California. Today, the market looks much different. The reign of flower has diminished. Consumer preferences towards concentrates has evolved. The public's interest in CBD is spiking. All while prices are dropping; laws are changing, and researchers are compiling. According to BDS Analytics, the following are the noteworthy trends of 2018.[35]

### Branded Products On The Rise

When the Colorado market took off in 2014, it was all about the flower. Jars of sticky buds grown for dispensaries and sold in Mason jars or plastic bags—in bulk and unbranded. Times have changed.

Now, market share is roughly tied at 48 percent each for branded products—edibles, most concentrates, and topicals—and unbranded products, including most flower and pre-rolls. And dollar sales growth through 2018 is led by branded products. In fact, in Colorado and Oregon, where year-over-year comparisons are useful (as opposed to California, which last year was a medical marketplace only), dollar sales of flower are down 6 percent through October of this year. Meanwhile, growth for edibles in the same states reached 21.5 percent through October; growth is even stronger among concentrates.[36]

Brand strength is about more than growth. When data was compared from the first half of 2017 with the same period in 2018, the researchers found the top ten brands in Colorado and Oregon command both higher prices on average and significantly more market share than competitors. But today's brand leaders may fall away with fresh competition. They found that in California, four new brands had gained a spot in the top ten in 2018 since the first half of 2017, with one of those managing to take the number one spot. Even the slightly older Colorado market saw the same kind of churn as California, with four new brands entering the top ten. Consumer spending in 2018 on legal cannabis exploded, growing nearly 30% to $11 billion.[37] Opportunity remains ripe in all states for adult-use (recreational) branded cannabis.

## Flower Prices Keep Falling

The price deflation in cannabis relates to unbranded flower, rather than branded products. This is great news for manufacturers of branded products—their most expensive ingredient, flower, continues to fall, even as their product prices remain roughly stable, or even rising.

## Big Alcohol Invests

Cannabis beverages have been on the receiving end of a fair bit of press in 2018. In August, beverage conglomerate Constellation Brands paid $4 billion for a 38 percent stake in Canopy Growth, a large Canadian cannabis cultivator. In addition, Molson Coors announced a partnership with HEXO; and ABI InBev with Tilray; and most recently, Moosehead Canada, announced a partnership with Sproutly to launch a line of cannabis-infused beverages.

When we examine adult-use states where year-over-year comparisons are useful—for example, Colorado and Oregon, but not California, which last year was a medical state—growth for (cannabis) beverages is solid, at 37 percent. But consumers in different states, for now, drink different kinds of beverages. What we are witnessing in the beverage market is the proliferation of products beyond large bottles of liquid. Powdered drinks, shots, and tea, for example, are making inroads. In California, sales of tea are rising fast and taking market share from the broad category of "cannabis beverages." In Colorado, water-soluble powders are expanding—decreasing the "liquid" beverage market share. In Oregon, sales of shots are nearly on par with drinks in that State's beverage market.[38]

With so much investment pouring into beverages, we are likely to witness more and more product innovation and evolution. Form factors beyond bottles or cans of liquid seem like an important part of the future.

## Robust Competition. Price Uniformity.

This year saw the rise of cannabis companies going big on low prices, especially in California's concentrates market. Due to the uplift in vape and oil cartridges, concentrates pricing today in California and other states are undergoing robust competition and experimentation. Expect to see more price uniformity, including lower overall prices for concentrates in 2020.[39]

CHAPTER EIGHT

# CANNABIS BRANDS: A CRITICAL REVIEW

*"The health and wellness industries have done a good job setting the bar for authentic influencer marketing. Now the nascent cannabis industry is primed to becoming the most fertile ground for influencer marketing yet. Genuine influencers are in a prime position to endorse products that have a clear and measurable efficacy. The onslaught of cannabis brands and numerous consumption methods provides a great opportunity for expert influencers to test and vet the daily stream of new products to hit the market. Brands that opt for a celebrity endorsement may get more marketing reach via their followers, but most consumers today understand those endorsements have been bought and sold."*
- MICHAEL BLATTER, FOUNDER, MIRRORBALL AGENCY

## WHAT MAKES A CANNABIS BRAND SUCCESSFUL?

This is perhaps the most interesting question of all and closely related to "Who is the cannabis consumer and what appeals to them?" To get closer to the answer, we need to look at a multitude of variables—much of which little data currently exists. These include form factor preference such as flower, oil, edibles, beverages, transdermal patches as well as sublingual strips among others. Customer segments such as age, race, socio-economic status, and usage pattern scenarios as well as distribution channels including recreational stores and medical dispensaries, play large roles in customer expectations and therefore, brand development.

Recreational consumers and medical patients often have varying perspectives on efficacy and means of consumption. Further, depending on their means of ingestion, both often have pre-conceived notions about products, how they're packaged, and under what circumstances they are to be used.

This variance across cannabis products and their use, requires us to take another look and ask, what works for the non-cannabis products that cannabis brands are mirroring? One would think medical cannabis products should look and be packaged differently from recreational cannabis products. Should cannabis sublingual strips look like Listerine® "breath-strips" or cannabis transdermal patches like Nicorette®? Should we be reinventing the wheel by creating new cannabis standards and conventions? Or build on the traditions and history of western consumer product goods packaging and nomenclature?

## Canna-Consumers Expectations

With the volume of competition that businesses face in most industries, it's never been more important to stand out and develop a unique identity and value proposition. While it's obviously important to offer a quality product and/or service, effective branding is often at the heart of the companies that thrive.

A brand is a perception someone holds about a person, a product, a service, an organization, a cause, or an idea. Brand building is the deliberate and skillful application of effort to create a desired perception in someone's mind. A few common characteristics of successful brands are:

### Audience Knowledge

The best brands have a thorough understanding of the demographics of their target market, what their interests are and how they communicate. Most businesses pursue a specific target audience. Understanding the target market is critical because it provides the overall identity of a brand while helping to create an organic, human connection between a brand and its audience.

### Uniqueness

Establishing a brand identity requires something distinctive. Creating an identity within a niche doesn't demand a revolutionary idea. It simply needs to have one special thing that differentiates it from the competition. It's possible to be "a one-trick pony" as long as that trick is unique and top of its class.

## Passion

While it's certainly possible to build a brand in the short-term without passion, it's almost impossible to sustain it in the long run. That passion leads to enthusiasm and genuine joy, which is infectious. Consumers often become just as enthusiastic about a product or service, leading to word of mouth advertising and referrals.

## Consistency

When consumers come back to a business for repeat sales, they usually expect to receive the same level of quality as they did the first time. No one wants to deal with a company they can't rely on for consistency. With so many industries being saturated with competitors, inconsistency is often enough of a reason for consumers to take their business elsewhere.

## Competitiveness

When it comes to the major players in any industry, none simply sit back and hope that their consumers will do the work for them. Instead, they tend to be the movers and shakers who work tirelessly toward building and optimizing their brand, going above and beyond consumer expectations.

## Exposure

Another big part of being recognized as a distinctive, successful brand is the ability to reach consumers through multiple channels. Obviously, larger companies have an advantage in gaining exposure because they usually have a bigger marketing budget and more existing connections.

What consumers and patients desire from a cannabis brand and its product(s) are based on both their expectations of what they want from the brand—balanced with what the brand actually promises. If a brand can deliver above and beyond its own promises and customer expectations, it will most likely be successful. In an effort to understand the general characteristics of success, we look to see where we can find similar business traits within the cannabis industry.

## What Attributes Make A Cannabis Brand Successful?

Cannabis brands are very much like other brands in that they have a specific function, purpose, and/or promote a unique perspective or attitude. What's missing? Scalability. Regardless of how much brand awareness and consistent a brand's products are, the current rules and regulations make it difficult for a cannabis company to profitably scale to a national level.

Because each state has its own rules and regulations making it difficult for consistent product and packaging from state to state, a decentralized business model is being forced upon those who are seeking to create a national brand. The fact that each state and/or region has developed its own taste preferences and palates over time, should come as no surprise since prohibition has created local cannabis economies.

That said, cannabis brand owners are left with growing, yet highly regulated markets to serve, bound by rules and regulations affecting their marketing strategies and tactics.

## Building National Brands

A major obstacle that every producer, processor, and or package marketer in the industry faces, is having a license in each state to grow and or process the cannabis required for their products—not to mention the restrictive cost of entry to acquire a license in each market. That said, there are many companies already finding solutions to this problem.

Many brands are forming licensing partnerships with local entities that are licensed to produce and/or process cannabis within their state. These entities have already invested in manufacturing facilities and now seek exclusive rights to sell the "branded" finished products within their individual states.

Savvy brand marketers are already segmenting their product SKU's to align with their customer's consumption habits; while others are perfecting their recipes—and intellectual property—so that it can be replicated, sourced and infused locally, then packaged and promoted according to brand specifications as well as local advertising and packaging regulatory requirements.

## Marketing Limitations

In addition to the many business and tax laws that stifle cannabis producers and processors, there are a number of issues at play that make creating and building a cannabis brand extremely difficult. With labeling, packaging, and advertising regulations constantly changing from state to state, marketing a product within a state—let alone on a national level—is essentially shooting at a moving target. Regulations including labeling, packaging, and advertising are just a few of the roadblocks from a branding and marketing perspective.

Below is a quick overview of the labeling, packaging, and advertising regulations in a few of the recreational states including Colorado, Oregon, Washington as well as California, the world's single largest medicinal market. With laws consistently changing, these rules and regulations will no doubt change or be revised.

## Labeling And Packaging Regulations

Proper cannabis labeling and packaging is a crucial component to staying in compliance with state guidelines. Cannabis brands must ensure that their packages are tamper-proof, childproof, and within accordance with local laws. Unfortunately, because the laws are constantly changing, businesses are forced to keep up with the costly and perpetual revisions to comply.

While each state has its own specific packaging laws, there are some general rules that cannabis brands must comply with. Prior to sale, cannabis products must be labeled, and in a tamper-evident package. Labels and packages of cannabis products typically need to meet the following requirements:

### Cannabis Labels Must Include:

- Manufacture date and source of cultivation and manufacture.
- For packages containing only dried flower, the net weight of cannabis.
- A warning if nuts and/or other known allergens are used.
- Active ingredients including, THC and CBD in mg per serving and servings per package.
- Clear indication, in bold type, that the product contains cannabis.
- Containers for edible marijuana products must be labeled with all ingredients.
- With specific wording including:
  - "Schedule I Controlled Substance."
  - "Keep Out Of Reach Of Children and Animals"
  - "The Intoxicating Effects Of This Product May Be Delayed By Up To Two Hours."
  - "This Product May Impair The Ability To Drive Or Operate Machinery. Please Use Extreme Caution."

## Cannabis Packaging Must Be:

- Opaque (Opacity by percentage depending on the State)
- Typically include the state's "THC Symbol"
- Re-closable if not intended for single-use
- Not be designed to appeal to children
- Child-resistant or placed into an "exit package" that is child-resistant
- Approved by each state's respective Liquor and Cannabis Board or equivalent

## Advertising Regulations

As the cannabis industry continues to grow at a rapid pace, it's overwhelming to keep up-to-date with the constantly changing state regulations. Advertising regulations are especially strict, as many marketing platforms restrict or outright ban cannabis advertisements due to the plant's federal status.

Much in the same way an alcohol company might be prevented from advertising in certain locations, cannabis advertising is highly regulated. The following is a list of general advertising regulations and restrictions required across different platforms including web, TV, radio, and general advertising.

## Cannabis Advertisers Must Not:

- Make deceptive, false, or misleading assertions or statements to a consumer.
- Utilize television advertising unless there is reliable evidence that no more than 30% of the audience for the program on which the advertising is to air is reasonably expected to be under the age of 21.
- Advertise on the radio unless the cannabis producer, processor, and/or retailer has reliable evidence that no more than 30% of the audience for the program on which the Advertising is to air is reasonably expected to be under the age of 21.
- Advertise in a print publication is prohibited unless the cannabis producer, processor, and/or retailer has reliable evidence that no more than 30% of the publication's readership is reasonably expected to be under the age of 21.
- Advertise on the internet unless the cannabis producer, processor and/or retailer have reliable evidence that no more than 30% of

the audience for the internet website is reasonably expected to be under the age of 21.

- Engage in advertising that specifically targets persons located outside the state.
- Utilize signage that asserts its products are safe because they are regulated by the State Licensing Authority or a Cannabis Testing Facility
- Include in any form of Advertising or signage any content that specifically targets individuals under the age of 21, including but not limited to cartoon characters or similar images.
- Engage in advertising via marketing directed towards location-based devices, including but not limited to cellular phones, unless the marketing is a mobile device application installed on the device by the owner of the device who is 21 years of age or older and includes a permanent and easy opt-out feature.
- Engage in advertising at, or in connection with, such an event unless the cannabis producer, processor and/or retailer has reliable evidence that no more than 30% of the audience at the event and/or viewing Advertising in connection with the event is reasonably expected to be under the age of 21.

To reiterate, these rules and regulations are in constant flux and differ from state to state, so be sure to check each specific state for its own guidelines.

With these branding and marketing guidelines in effect, one can see how handcuffed a cannabis brand can be when seeking to build a national brand. Different states require different packages and labels, different advertising tactics, different tax regulations, and even different testing specifications for pesticides and microbials.

Perhaps this is why most brands have matured at similar rates and each region has developed in similar ways. From local farms and growers direct to their friends and distributors. Over time, a broader, more diverse customer base called for a more professional, 'consumer packaged good' product where the local grower no longer sold the product directly; rather the customer purchased the package because of its "shelf appeal" and came back for more—if it lived up to their expectations.

## THE EVOLUTION OF A CANNABIS BRAND

Since the legalization of cannabis, we have seen a number of branding strategies and trends. By this I mean, a clear pattern that allows us to see and group an evolution of development in branding and packaging across the sector. While this may not seem so surprising over time, we can see a rapid and distinct evolution of cannabis brands since legalization, starting with local farm-based brands moving to CPG type brands and most recently, luxury, celebrity and nostalgia-based brands. This is most likely due to the fact that professional marketers are entering the industry and uplifting it as a whole by building new brands and creating awareness and acceptance.

There's no doubt there will be an evolution of brands as medical and recreational rules and regulations change from state to state and eventually, at the federal level. The evolution of brands from farm-based (Wave 1); to derivatives and or cannabis-related names (Wave 2); transforming into more CPG packaging with names evoking post-prohibition themes such as "Zoots" and "Legal", as well as other brands, focused on their healing qualities and efficacy such as Apothecanna, among others (Wave 3). More recently, there has been a slew of celebrity-based cannabis brands including Tommy Chong, Bob Marley, Snoop Dogg, Willie Nelson, Whoopi Goldberg, Rhianna, Wiz Khalifa, The Game, Melissa Etheridge, just to name a few (Wave 4).

## The Celebrity Effect

Celebrities have long been used as the face of brands. Since the early 1900s, brands have been leveraging celebrities to promote and sell their products. From Humphrey Bogart and Lauren Bacall advertising Cigarillos to modern-day brands like Nike, Apple, T-Mobile and Beats By Dre leveraging celebrities to endorse and build their brands.

Celebrity endorsements have and can reap huge rewards for a brand. Yet they have numerous pitfalls that a brand should consider before associating themselves with a celebrity, let alone building their brand upon a celebrity's persona.

Today, brand ambassadors are the norm. Celebrity endorsements and celebrity-owned start-ups and ventures are not uncommon. Examples abound and include Jessica Alba, Gwyneth Paltrow, Ashton Kutcher, David Beckham, among others.

There are a number of advantages to using celebrities in advertising, whether running print, Internet, radio, or television commercials. The key for brands is making sure the celebrity is relevant and has broad appeal. Popular celebrities often work best because they naturally generate lots of attention. Despite their fan-base, celebrities are most effective if they promote products and/or services they are most likely to use. In other words, they must be plausible consumers.

The affinity consumers have for certain celebrities can greatly influence their purchases. People may have the attitude, "If the product is good enough for her, it's good enough for me." This philosophy is often the impetus behind advertisements for makeup, skin creams, hair products, and attire. Consumers want the wavy hair of a local celebrity, for example. Hence, they purchase the brand that the celebrity uses to achieve her hair's fullness and bounce. Essentially, the testimonial of the celebrity adds instant credibility to a company's product.

Celebrity endorsements can improve ad recall, according to researchers Jagdish Agrawal and Wagner Kamakura. Celebrities in advertising build brand awareness and they build it much more quickly than traditional types of advertising. Brand awareness measures the percentage of people who are familiar with a particular brand.

Some companies use celebrities to position or re-position their brands. Product positioning is placing a company's products in the best possible light in the minds of a specific target group.

One challenge brands face is finding new users for their products. Celebrities appeal to current customers, as well as those who have never tried a brand's product(s). Yet even if a celebrity is a good fit for a brand, leveraging one for endorsements has its own set of possible risks.

Celebrities are people, and people make mistakes. And when they do, they can affect the brands they endorse. In 2009, Tiger Woods' public image crumbled after his infidelity. General Motors, Gillette, Accenture, and Gatorade dropped Tiger to avoid negative perception. While Nike stuck around and lost customers.

At the height of Tiger Woods' popularity, he endorsed over ten companies at once. When a celebrity works with so many companies, the celebrity's credibility may suffer. People may feel that the celebrity will endorse anything to make a buck.

Consumers may focus on the celebrity, not the product. This is a particular danger when celebrities endorse multiple products at the same time. David Beckham endorses a number of companies, which feature him prominently in print advertising. That said, his image as the focal point of the advertisements he's in devalues the product(s) around him.

High-profile celebrities partnering with private companies for mutual gain is hardly a new concept. In the cannabis industry, however, it's one that's gaining traction. Many cannabis companies have inked deals with celebrities that have long been associated with cannabis. Other celebrities have started up their own product lines, opting to do it their way instead of partnering with established firms.

Among the relationships forged to date include Tommy Chong's partnership with Pueblo, Colorado-based Marisol Therapeutics. Seattle-based Privateer Holdings struck a deal with reggae legend Bob Marley's estate in 2014; and rapper Snoop Dogg licensed his name to a line of vaporizers manufactured by Grenco Science as well as with LivWell, one of the largest retailers and cultivators in Colorado for his "Leafs By Snoop" brand.

> *"It's really been the partnership with Snoop that has taken us to the next level and separated us from other brands in the market."*
>
> - TIM PATENAUDE, VP, GRENCO SCIENCE

The proliferation of cannabis-related businesses means that business-owners are seeking new ways to differentiate their brand and stand out in the minds of consumers.

So, who are the celebrities? Many have licensed their names and likeness to the cannabis industry through product endorsements; as well as investing in their own cannabis brands themselves. Here's an abbreviated list of recent celebrity activity in the cannabis sector:

### Willie Nelson

Country music legend, poet and activist Willie Nelson, announced his personal brand of cannabis. Says a company representative, "the new products are created to envelop Willie's personal morals and convictions."

Photo Courtesy: Willie's Reserve

### Bob Marley

Billionaire Peter Thiel invested in Privateer Holdings, a firm with several investments in legal cannabis, including the partnership with Bob Marley's family called Marley Natural, "the world's first global cannabis brand."

Photo Courtesy: Marley Natural

According to a company, press release Marley Natural will, "offer premium cannabis products that honor the life and legacy of Bob Marley as well as his belief in the benefits of cannabis."

---

*"It's a wellness brand. It's a lifestyle brand. It's not just focused on a very specific aspect of cannabis, which I think is maybe a little bit more what the stereotype would lead to."*
- TAHIRA REHMATULLAH, FORMER GM OF MARLEY NATURAL

---

Marley Natural plans to enter the market growing and selling cannabis strains in Colorado, Oregon, and Washington, where recreational is already legal. Non-cannabis smoking accessories and non-infused body care products are available currently in all 50 states.

### Wiz Khalifa

The Grammy-nominated, chart-topping rapper has his own Khalifa Kush, sold in San Jose, CA. Khalifa gets an unlimited supply of the Indica-dominant hybrid, in exchange for lending his name to the cut. He also partnered with RAW papers, a smart way to expand the reach of the RAW brand.

Photo Courtesy: Mario Anzuoni – Reuters

### Snoop Dogg

Recently, Snoop launched in a limited-time exclusive relationship with LivWell, one of the largest pot shop operators and cultivators in Colorado. "Leafs By Snoop" cannabis products are made under a Colorado marijuana licensee, Beyond Broadway, which does business as LivWell and will grow the brand's

Photo Courtesy: Dope Magazine

flower and manufacture its edibles and concentrates. What's more important, is we're not only seeing the emergence of celebrity marijuana brands, we are seeing these brands forge strategic partnerships with recreational stores and dispensaries, growers and processors, as well as statewide distributors.

Snoop isn't the only rapper branching out into cannabis-related accessories. Rapper The Game has also designed a vaporizer and Lil Wayne has a line of cigars—called Bogey Cigars targeted at cannabis smokers.

### Tommy Chong

One of the godfathers of the 'stoner' culture, Tommy Chong, manages to capitalize on his relationship with weed culture recently by licensing his name to a new product called, "Tommy Chong's Smoke Swipe" - a line of dry wipes meant to eliminate the odor of cannabis or tobacco smoke from smokers' clothes. After recently competing on the reality show, "Dancing with the Stars", Chong is a household name more than ever before.

Photo Courtesy: Koi Sojer

Celebrities are escalating their cannabis commercialism beyond paraphernalia. For the first time, artists, directors, and even authors are directly lending their likeness and name to cannabis products.

There's always been "cannabis celebrities" including Tommy Chong, Jorge Cervantes, Jack Herer, Ed Rosenthal among others. Today, there are television, movie, and pop stars participating at cannabis festivals and events, as well as licensing their names to various canna-brands. Think Seth Rogan, Whoopi Goldberg, and Sarah Silverman, just to name a few.

An example of cannabis making its way into mass media is The Wonderful Pistachios commercial featuring Snoop Dogg. Such suggestive spots pass over those heads that don't "get it"—while those that do, appreciate it that much more.

> "What's more important, is we're not only seeing the emergence of celebrity marijuana brands, we're seeing these brands forge strategic partnerships with recreational stores and dispensaries, growers and processors, as well as statewide distributors."
> - CHRISTOPHER GALVIN, CEO, HYPUR VENTURES

A consumer reacts better to an ad when it gives them an incentive, a personal benefit, rather than one that is a hard sell—and celebrities bring more than a hard sell.

Celebrity marketing has a long history including baseball gloves with players' signatures or Arnold Palmer's preferred golf clubs. The appeal is both the idea that a buyer has a shared experience with a celebrity and that a celebrity knows what constitutes top quality.

Perhaps nostalgia plays into the picture as well. As America's roughly 78 million baby boomers reach their 60s, there is no doubt that nostalgia will most likely play an even more integral role in marketing than it already does. At a time when technology is advancing at an ever-increasing pace, legendary brands and institutions are toppling left and right. Nothing feels durable or lasting anymore. As consumers, we protectively cling to those brands that have not only endured from our childhood but bring us back to relive the memories of that simpler, more stable time—and celebrities such as Chong, Nelson, Snoop, and others feed that need.

Despite the saturation of celebrity news and gossip, there was no sign that the public's appetite for celebrity has diminished and certainly, marketers appear to be employing them as much as, or even more, than ever before.

As cannabis moves to mainstream and additional states legalize, there will be more and more business opportunities for celebrity endorsements. Some predict there will be a handful of legacy brands, between the Marley family, the Chong endorsement, the Jimi Hendrix family, and the Snoop Dogg group. Time will tell.

*"The businesses who leave the pot leaf out of the brand identity are more often taken seriously by both the consumer and the state regulators."*
- LINDSAY GATZ, VONROCKO DESIGN

## What's In A Brand Name And Color?

It's a curious thing that a mere brand name can persuade us to engage emotionally with a product or company. Sometimes, we even develop an unwitting loyalty or long-lasting aversion to a brand, though we might know little about it. How is this possible?

Naming is a complex, messy blend of science and art, a fusion of unstructured creativity and meticulous logic. The idea phase is elaborate in which inspiration comes from abstract concepts – topical themes, sounds, different languages, and more, and literally, hundreds of names can be generated for each project. But if creating names can be challenging, selecting one name from many is even more so.

Since most companies start small with an emphasis on the idea for the product or service rather than the brand, the name arises as an afterthought. There is a strong likelihood that the name will be chosen on emotive grounds rather than on solid scientific research. Since every company needs a name and because one name is just as good as another, why not pluck it out of the air? And often it is.

Some criteria raised in brand name research as factors that affect the recall and recognition of brands are as follows:

- Simple so that they are easy to understand, pronounce and spell.
- Vivid in imagery so that the mnemonics present strong memory cues.
- Familiar so that much of the information is already stored in the mind.
- Distinctive so as not to be confused with other brands.

These guidelines are not necessarily mutually compatible, as it may be difficult to find names that are simple, vivid in imagery, familiar, and distinctive. There is some evidence to suggest that if the mind has to work harder to understand and recognize the name, it will be more likely to be retained in the long-lasting memory than a familiar name that fails to become lodged. Familiar words may facilitate brand recall, but distinctive words work better at building brand recognition. An example of this in the cannabis space is the brand Avitas. Strangely familiar, this is Sativa spelled backward.

> "There is evidence to suggest that if the mind has to work harder to understand and recognize the name, it will be more likely to be retained in the long-lasting memory than a familiar name that fails to become lodged."
>
> - L.J. Shrum, Researcher: Phonetic Symbolism

## Different Types Of Names

Linguists are often consulted to brainstorm appropriate names for brands, products, and companies. Indeed, there are a number of popular linguistic devices that can be used to form effective brand names, such as the phonetic alliteration in Coca-Cola or the morphological elements in Craftmatic or semantic allusions in a brand name like Nike.

Semantic metaphors conveying visible, easy to understand meanings ensure that iconic brand names like Apple and Jaguar continue to be popular. But even brand names built on solid naming principles can fail. It turns out that the mere letters and sounds used in a brand name can have a curious impact on its reception by the public, persuading us into developing an emotional bond with the product.

Based on studies of popular brand names and experiments involving made-up brand names, linguists and psychologists have found some interesting patterns which, if followed to the letter, so to speak, may well have an impact on future trends in branding.

A study by Tina M. Lowrey and L. J. Shrum[1] on phonetic symbolism and brand names suggests that consonants and vowels in themselves can convey symbolic meaning, with certain sounds being more positive and others more negative in emphasizing certain properties and characteristics of a product.

## The Importance Of Color In Branding

It's likely because personal preference, experiences, upbringing, cultural differences, and context often muddy the effect individual colors have on us.

But there's still plenty to learn and consider if we humbly accept that concrete answers aren't a guarantee. The key is to look for practical ways to make decisions about color. Substantial research shows why color matters and how color plays a pivotal role in all our visual experiences.

Although the olfactory sense was a human being's most important source of input in the pre-historic era, sight became our most important means of survival. Furthermore, as hunters and gatherers in the early days of our evolution, we experienced a variety of colors and forms in the landscape. This has become part of our genetic code.

In our current state of evolution, vision is the primary source for our experiences. Current marketing research has reported that approximately 80 percent of what we assimilate through the senses, is visual. Many studies[2] have classified consumer responses and psychological properties to individual colors as called out below:

## The Psychological Properties Of The 11 Basic Colors:

### Red

*Positive: Physicality, courage, strength, warmth, energy, excitement*
*Negative: Defiance, aggression, visual impact, strain*

Being the longest wavelength, red is a powerful color. Although not technically the most visible, it has the property of appearing to be closer than it is and therefore grabs our attention first, hence its universal effectiveness in traffic lights and stop signs. Its effect is physical: it stimulates us and raises the pulse rate, giving the impression that time is passing faster than it is. It relates to the masculine principle and can activate the "fight or flight" instinct.

## Blue

*Positive: Intelligence, trust, efficiency, serenity, logic, reflection, calm*
*Negative: Coldness, aloofness, lack of emotion, unfriendliness*

Blue is the color of the mind and is essentially soothing. It affects us mentally, rather than the physical reaction we have to red. Strong blues will stimulate clear thought and lighter, softer blues will calm the mind and aid concentration. It is serene and mentally calming. It is the color of clear communication. In research, blue tends to be the world's favorite color.

## Yellow

*Positive: Optimism, confidence, self-esteem, friendliness, creativity*
*Negative: Irrationality, fear, emotional fragility, depression, anxiety*

The yellow wavelength is relatively long and stimulating. In this case, the stimulus is emotional, therefore yellow is the strongest color, psychologically. The right yellow will lift our spirits and our self-esteem; it is the color of confidence and optimism. Too much of it, or the wrong tone in relation to the other tones, can give rise to fear and anxiety.

## Green

*Positive: Harmony, balance, love, reassurance, equilibrium, peace*
*Negative: Boredom, stagnation, blandness, enervation*

Green strikes the eye in such a way as to require no adjustment whatever and is, therefore, restful. Being in the center of the spectrum, it is the color of balance: a more important concept than many people realize. When the world around us contains plenty of green, it indicates the presence of water, so we are reassured by the color on a primitive level.

## Violet

*Positive: Spiritual awareness, vision, luxury, authenticity, truth, quality*
*Negative: Introversion, decadence, suppression, inferiority*

The shortest wavelength is violet, often described as purple. It takes awareness to a higher level of thought, even into the realms of spiritual values. It is highly introversive and encourages deep contemplation or meditation. It has associations with royalty and usually communicates the finest possible quality.

## Orange
*Positive:* Physical comfort, food, warmth, sensuality, passion
*Negative:* Deprivation, frustration, frivolity, immaturity

Since it is a combination of red and yellow, orange is stimulating and the reaction to it is a combination of the physical and the emotional. It focuses our minds on issues of physical comfort such as food, warmth, shelter, and sensuality. It is a "fun" color. Negatively, it might focus on the exact opposite: deprivation. This is particularly likely when warm orange is used with black.

## Pink
*Positive:* Physical tranquility, nurture, warmth, femininity, love, sexuality
*Negative:* Inhibition, emasculation, physical weakness

Being a hue of red, pink also affects us physically, but it soothes, rather than stimulates. Pink is a powerful color, psychologically. It represents the feminine principle and survival of the species and is nurturing and physically soothing. Too much pink is physically draining and can be somewhat emasculating.

## Grey
*Positive:* Psychological neutrality
*Negative:* Lack of confidence, dampness, depression, lethargy

Pure grey is the only color that has no direct psychological properties. It is, however, quite suppressive. A virtual absence of color is depressing and when the world turns grey, we are instinctively conditioned to draw in and prepare for hibernation. Unless the precise tone is right, grey has a dampening effect on other colors used with it.

## Black
*Positive:* Sophistication, glamour, security, emotional safety, efficiency
*Negative:* Oppression, coldness, menace, heaviness

Black is all colors, totally absorbed. The psychological implications of that are considerable. It creates protective barriers, as it absorbs all the energy coming towards you, and it enshrouds the personality. Black is essentially an absence of light since no wavelengths are reflected and it can therefore be menacing; many people are afraid of the dark. Positively, it communicates absolute clarity, with no fine nuances.

## White
*Positive: Hygiene, sterility, purity, simplicity, sophistication, efficiency*
*Negative: Sterility, coldness, barriers, unfriendliness, elitism*

Just as black is total absorption; white is total reflection. In effect, it reflects the full force of the spectrum into our eyes. Thus, it also creates barriers, but differently from black, and it is often a strain to look at. White is purity and, like black, uncompromising; it is clean, hygienic, and sterile. The concept of sterility can also be negative. Visually, white gives a heightened perception of space.

## Brown
*Positive: Seriousness, warmth, nature, earthiness, reliability, support*
*Negative: Lack of humor, heaviness, lack of sophistication*

Brown usually consists of red and yellow, with a large percentage of black. Consequently, it has much of the same seriousness as black but is warmer and softer. It has elements of the red and yellow properties. Brown has associations with the earth and the natural world. It is a solid, reliable color and most people find it quietly supportive, more positively than the ever-popular black, which is suppressive rather than supportive.

The truth is that color is too dependent on personal experiences to be universally translated to specific feelings. There are, however, broader messaging patterns to be found in color perceptions.

In a study titled *"Impact Of Color On Marketing"*,[3] researchers found that up to 90 percent of snap judgments made about products can be based on color alone. Other studies show4 the role that color plays in branding is more contextual—for example, does the color "fit" with what is being sold or the context it's being used in?

A study titled *"Exciting Red And Competent Blue"*[4] also confirms that purchasing intent is greatly affected by colors due to their effect on how a brand is perceived. Colors influence how customers view the "personality" of the brand. Who, for example, would want to buy a Harley Davidson motorcycle if they didn't get the feeling that Harleys were rugged and cool?

Additional studies[5] have revealed our brains prefer immediately recognizable brands, which makes color an important element when creating a brand identity. It's important for new brands to pick colors that ensure differentiation from entrenched competitors. Most importantly perhaps is the need for additional context, such as *how* and *why* you're positioning against a direct competitor, and how you're using color to achieve that goal.

When it comes to picking the "right" color, predicting consumer reaction to color appropriateness is far more important than the individual color itself. If Harley owners buy the product in order to feel rugged, colors that work best will play to that emotion.

Psychologist and Stanford professor Jennifer Aaker has conducted studies on this very topic, and her paper titled *"Dimensions of Brand Personality"*[6] points out five core dimensions that play a role in a brand's personality:

- Sincerity
- Excitement
- Competence
- Sophistication
- Ruggedness

Brands can sometimes cross between two traits but are mostly dominated by one. While certain colors do broadly align with specific traits (e.g., brown with ruggedness, purple with sophistication, and red with excitement), nearly every academic study[7] on colors and branding will tell you that it's far more important for colors to support the personality you want to portray instead of trying to align with stereotypical color associations.

Consider the inaccuracy of making broad statements such as "green means calm." The context is absent: sometimes green is used to brand environmental issues, like Seventh Generation®, but other times it's meant to brand financial spaces, such as Mint®.

And while brown may be useful for a rugged appeal, when positioned in another context, brown can be used to create a warm, inviting feeling or to stir your appetite.

There are no clear-cut guidelines for choosing your brand's colors. "It depends" is a frustrating answer, but it's the truth. It's really about the context you're working in. It's the feeling, mood, and image that your brand or product creates that matters most.

---

*"Most academic studies on colors and branding will tell you that it's far more important for colors to support the personality you want to portray instead of trying to align with stereotypical color associations."*

- Jared Mirsky, Founder, Wick and Mortar

---

## Color Trends for Men And Women

One of the more interesting examinations of this topic is Joe Hallock's work on *"Color Assignment."*[8] Hallock's data showcases some clear preferences in certain colors across gender with most of his respondents from Western societies. The most notable points in his images are the supremacy of blue and green across both genders and the disparity between groups on purple.

22 percent of the male participants gave their least favorite color vote to purple, which is very interesting because 20 percent of males stated that purple represented courage and bravery. This shows some inconsistency between the members of the male participants. Women, on the other hand, only gave 8 percent of their vote to purple as their least favorite color. And 34 percent of women associated purple with courage or bravery. This gender difference is interesting, and I believe it's caused by cultural changes in color association over time. Other studies from the 1950s and 60s note 'dignity' as one of the adjectives in defining purple. This may be related to the "Purple Heart Medal" which is given by the US Military to any member who is wounded or killed in the line of duty; whereas purple today might be associated with freedom, openness, and perhaps even the LGBTQ community.[9]

It's important to note that one's environment—and especially cultural perception—plays a strong role in dictating color appropriateness for gender, which in turn can influence individual choices. Here are Hallock's findings:

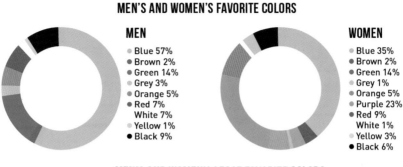

### MEN'S AND WOMEN'S FAVORITE COLORS

**MEN**
- Blue 57%
- Brown 2%
- Green 14%
- Grey 3%
- Orange 5%
- Red 7%
- White 7%
- Yellow 1%
- Black 9%

**WOMEN**
- Blue 35%
- Brown 2%
- Green 14%
- Grey 1%
- Orange 5%
- Purple 23%
- Red 9%
- White 1%
- Yellow 3%
- Black 6%

### MEN'S AND WOMEN'S LEAST FAVORITE COLORS

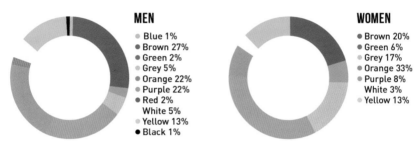

**MEN**
- Blue 1%
- Brown 27%
- Green 2%
- Grey 5%
- Orange 22%
- Purple 22%
- Red 2%
- White 5%
- Yellow 13%
- Black 1%

**WOMEN**
- Brown 20%
- Green 6%
- Grey 17%
- Orange 33%
- Purple 8%
- White 3%
- Yellow 13%

Additional research in studies on color perception and color preferences[10] show that when it comes to shades, tints, and hues,[11] men generally prefer bold colors while women prefer softer colors. Also, men were more likely to select shades of colors as their favorites (colors with black added), whereas women are more receptive to tints of colors (colors with white added).

Although this is a hotly debated issue in color theory, I've never understood why. Brands can easily work outside of gender stereotypes—in fact, I'd argue many have been rewarded for doing so because they break expectations. "Perceived appropriateness" shouldn't be so rigid as to assume a brand or product can't succeed because the colors don't match surveyed tastes.[12]

After reviewing numerous studies on color and the related psychological effects on consumers including Hallock's work on color preferences and brands, it's not surprising that cannabis brands are primarily blue and green. The combined demand for blue and greens by both females and males overlaid with brand promises of harmony, balance, peace, reassurance, and equilibrium make sense in conveying the natural essence and benefits of a cannabis-based product. But how do they differentiate their brand under these circumstances?

Hallock's summary on the disparity between groups relative to the color purple is quite interesting since there are a number of violet, lavender, and purple-based brands within the cannabis space. Violet is known to appeal to our senses of spiritual awareness and vision, as well as evoke feelings of luxury, authenticity, truth, and quality.

While a potential branding strategy leveraging a violet-based color might work on many levels, research shows that 22 percent of men choose purple to be their least favorite color. On the contrary, 23 percent of women choose purple as their favorite color. With that disparity, a brand owner might best not choose purple if seeking to appeal to men.

And while much research still needs to be done on cannabis consumers and their preferences, one question already exists—do violet-based cannabis brands appeal more to women or men?

The chart below bundles legal cannabis brands from California, Colorado, Oregon, and Washington by color. This allows one to review the newly forming canna-brand landscape and better understand how and where products can differentiate themselves.

## BRAND DIFFERENTIATORS AND CRITICAL CHARACTERISTICS

So, what are those characteristics that differentiate a brand? Brand differentiation happens when a product or service matches superior performance with an important customer benefit. A customer benefit is either something tangible or intangible that the market needs or values.

A company's brand differentiation strategy tends to evolve from its strengths. Organizations that are good at innovation, for instance, typically introduce products that become category leaders. A category leader is a brand that consumers first think of when seeking a particular benefit. For example, certain retailers are known for their "low prices," while others are known for "personalized service." There are many benefits that consumers value and look for when purchasing a product. Below are the most common ways brands create differentiation:

### Product Features

A product that solves problems faster or solves the same problem cheaper is worth paying more for. Hyundai has positioned itself as a car company that offers "more vehicle" for the money.

## Manufacturing Process

How the product is made can be a great way to set your brand apart from the competition. In today's economy where most products have become commodities, the "secret ingredient" or "proprietary technology" can definitely make the difference. Lululemon®, a well-known Canadian manufacturer of yoga-inspired apparel, has built its success on the proprietary Luon®, a fabric that provides shape retention and great stretching capabilities

## Performance

Execution is another great product attribute that can be used to separate your brand from the competition. BMW makes great use of this concept by positioning their cars as "The ultimate driving machine." Cervelo's dedication to designing and building aerodynamic bikes is what helped the brand carve a distinctive niche in the super-competitive race bike segment dominated by much bigger players.

## Design

Attractive, unique product design is a very effective way to differentiate. Apple is constantly pursuing this strategy that reflects in the entire assortment, from iPods to MacBooks.

These are just a few examples of how product-based differentiation can be achieved. There are unlimited options a company can employ, depending on its capital, capabilities, rules, and restrictions.

> *"It's those brands that differentiate their story and messaging by visually tailoring their communications and delivering them in a manner that's relevant to their consumers that will be recognized and rewarded."*
>
> - LINDSAY TOPPING, DIRECTOR OF MARKETING, DIXIE ELIXIRS

As momentum for cannabis legalization grows nationally, the commercialization of cannabis is no longer a pipe dream. In fact, it is becoming a reality right before our eyes, providing companies with the opportunity to build an enduring national, perhaps global brand.

All brands are bound to play within the rules and regulations of their respective states and municipalities. They must seek creative ways to make the laws work best for their businesses and more effectively than their competitors in order to succeed.

The number one critical success factor is consistency. A readily available product with a consistent look, feel, dose and flavor is crucial. While consistency might sound inflexible, it is not meant to be. Through consistency, one can better chart a brand roadmap that's in-line and suits the customer's needs. The cannabis sector is forever shifting. The fewer moving parts in the equation, the easier it is to contain and control the variables.

Calling out specific attributes is difficult as canna-products cross a wide range of form factors, demographics and usage scenarios. Why do we expect to see cannabis-infused edibles packaged like other baked goods and candies? Or cannabis-infused transdermal patches packaged like Band Aids®? Or cannabis-infused sublingual slips packaged like Listerine® breath strips?

The answer is: We have pre-conceived notions about brands and their products; how they're packaged and under what circumstances we use them. A child-resistant cap or tamper-proof package immediately puts us at ease and makes us feel assured about our safety and consumption.

Brands and color are inextricably linked because color offers an instantaneous method for conveying meaning and message without words. Color is the visual component people remember most about a brand followed closely by shapes/symbols then numbers and finally words.

Understanding customer needs is at the heart of every marketing strategy. That said, brands spend too little time identifying the right context for their message. All brands have a clear idea of their audience: identifying, understanding, and segmenting customers underpins every marketing strategy. But how much effort is spent uncovering a brand's ideal target context—the times, places, and moments when a message will resonate best?

Aligning marketing strategies with emotion has already proven to be successful but tapping into fond memories can be an invaluable tactic, especially for engaging millennials. From fast food and breakfast cereals to gaming systems and everything in between, smart brands are engaging through retro roots—known as nostalgia marketing. Perhaps why celebrity brands have had much traction in the cannabis space appealing to young current consumers as well as older consumers harkening back to their high school and college years.

Differentiation may quite possibly be the top priority in brand development. In today's competitive business environment, simply being better than other brands no longer creates a sustainable advantage. A brand must be different.

Creating a "different" brand that's unique and yet relatable, is key. Not unlike most other branded categories, cannabis brands often fall into fourteen general categories or brand archetypes.

## THE 14 CANNABIS BRAND ARCHETYPES

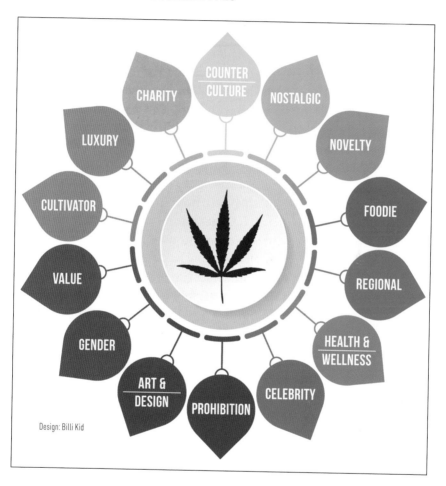

Design: Billi Kid

As momentum for cannabis legalization grows nationally, the commercialization of cannabis is no longer a pipe dream. In fact, it is becoming a reality right before our eyes, providing companies the opportunity to build enduring national, perhaps global brands.

Brand archetypes categorize universal patterns we intuitively know; helping us to quickly understand a brand's point of view. And as such, they are an effective marketing "short-cut" embodying common elements.

Applying these elements to a brand, helps potential customers identify and understand it—instantly.

While all brands are bound to play within the rules and regulations of their respective states and municipalities, they must seek creative ways to make the laws work best for their businesses and more effectively than their competitors in order to succeed.

The number one critical success factor is consistency. A readily available product with a consistent look, feel, dose and flavor is crucial. While consistency might sound inflexible, it is not meant to be. Through consistency, one can better chart a brand roadmap that's in-line and suits the customer's needs. The cannabis sector is forever shifting. The fewer moving parts in the equation, the easier it is to contain and control the variables.

Calling out specific attributes is difficult as canna-products cross a wide range of form factors, demographics and usage scenarios. Why do we expect to see cannabis-infused edibles packaged like other baked goods and candies? Or cannabis-infused transdermal patches packaged like Band Aids®? Or cannabis-infused sublingual slips packaged like Listerine® breath strips?

The answer is: We have pre-conceived notions about brands and their products; how they're packaged and under what circumstances we use them. A child-resistant cap or tamper-proof package immediately puts us at ease and makes us feel assured about our safety and consumption.

> *Color is the visual component people remember most about a brand followed closely by shapes, symbols, numbers, and finally, words.*

Brands and color are inextricably linked because color offers an instantaneous method for conveying meaning and message without words. Color is the visual component people remember most about a brand followed closely by shapes, symbols, numbers, and finally words.

In a world where appropriation and mashups abound, it's no surprise that brand archetypes often overlap and are not mutually exclusive. Meaning, many brands span one or more brand archetype categories.

## The 14 Cannabis Brands Archetypes

### Counter-Culture

Counter-culture brands are those brands that serve consumers who often define themselves and their activities through rebellion (i.e. not belonging to a certain group) counter cultures simply "feed the flames" of consumer culture by creating a whole new set of goods for "rebel consumers"

## Nostalgic

Research shows that nostalgia gives our lives a sense of continuity and meaning as we get older. As we age, we all develop fond memories of our younger days, from the food we ate to the games we played, to the music we listened to. It's no surprise many cannabis brands use nostalgia as a brand pillar.

## Novelty

When a consumer encounters a novel image tied to a brand, they are driven to learn more about it. They compare it to existing information: is it new and how does it fit into what they already know? Novelty is a powerful tool; but, it's also a dangerous one. The key to using novelty to attract interest is to make sure it's a new expression of something the brand always stood for. A great example of a novelty brand is "Impeachmints" manufactured by Evergreen Herbal.

## Foodie

Understanding how farm and food relate is essential for marketing to this sought-after demographic. Marketing to Foodies requires staying up to date on the latest trends across the food world. Given the increased importance everyone is placing on food, marketers would be wise to stay current. With the interconnectedness of food culture to almost everything, the relationship with cannabis is clear.

## Regional

A regional brand reflects the culture and qualities of a particular appellation or terroir. Examples of cannabis strains boasting their geographic origin include Maui Wowie, Durban Poison, Acapulco Gold, and Humboldt OG, to name a few. That said, it's no surprise that many brands seek to capture and leverage these nuanced, regional, and cultural qualities into their brands.

## Health And Wellness

Health and wellness brands have honed their messages putting customer's well-being front and center. They typically focus on product quality, efficacy, benefits, and an overall balanced lifestyle. Successful brands in the health and wellness space do best when they provide their customers with aspirational content, as well as easy access to information and tools that allow them to embrace a healthy lifestyle.

### Celebrity

Celebrity branding is a marketing strategy used by leveraging the celebrity's social status or fame to help promote a product or service. Brands use celebrities in hopes that the persona and image of the celebrity will be passed on to the product(s) and/or the brand associated with the celebrity.

### Prohibition

Prohibition refers to the banning of the manufacture, storage (whether in barrels or in bottles), transportation, sale, possession, and consumption of alcoholic beverages. The word is also used to refer to a period of time during which such bans are enforced. Today, many cannabis brands are connecting the concept of alcohol prohibition to cannabis legalization. Examples of these prohibition brands include Toast, PR%FF, Zoots, Lowell Herb Co. among others.

### Art And Design

The relationship between art and commerce has always been filled with anxiety. The diminishing impact of traditional advertising has caused brands to seek new ways to capture the attention of consumers. Artists and the art market have taught us how valuable a brand can become leveraging art and artists. Seattle based Saints Joints is a perfect example of a cannabis brand working with artists to create collectible, limited editioned box packaging.

### Gender Focused

While statistics tell us the majority of cannabis consumers are male, the female and LGBTQ segments are an under-developed opportunity—possibly the number one opportunity for those who understand how sexuality, gender, and political perspective resonate in this segment. While many have tried to "pink it and shrink it", we certainly know that strategy hasn't worked for brands outside of the cannabis industry.

### Value

A "budget brand" is a brand whose major selling point is its low price and/

or value offering. Often, but not always; that may mean lower quality. Since COVID-19, there has been an increase in larger, pre-packaged product offerings, such as pre-ground flower in pouches—rolling papers included.

### Cannabis Cultivator

Cultivator brands have taken off with the interest and development in strains, terpenes, and cannabinoids. Cookies is a perfect example of how a brand can grow from strain genetics. Well known cultivators and cultivator brands include Sherbinskis, Cookies, Exotics, Ed Rosenthal, among others.

### Luxury

Luxury cannabis brands are those that comprise associations of high price, high quality, beauty, rarity, and perhaps, even a degree of non-functionality. One of the best examples of a cannabis luxury brand is the Leira Cannagar, called out by Forbes Magazine as a "Gourmet Ultra Luxury Cannagar."

### Charity And Social Justice

People's willingness to devote their loyalty and money to a cause is directly influenced by the positive connection they have with a brand. The right image, personality, and tone of voice create an identity that your customers (and donors) can relate to, which leads to more sales and better fundraising. A great example of a cannabis charity brand is California's GIVE.

## Summary

How consumers attach themselves to a brand is based on the brand's ability to tell its story to its customer. A health and wellness brand should not brand and market its product in the same way a recreational brand focused on rebellion would. Different customer segments demand different products, whether real or perceived. It behooves brands to creatively leverage the most recognizable brand archetype elements in order to effectively and efficiently convey who they are and what they stand for. It's those brands that best differentiate and communicate, that will be recognized and rewarded.

CHAPTER NINE

# TAKING CUES FROM OTHER INDUSTRIES

## BEST PRACTICES AND PERTINENT PROCESSES

As the momentum continues, there are clear ties to other industries and lots of information, processes, and best practices to leverage. The cannabis industry utilizes products and knowledge from soil, fertilizer, and nutrient companies, lighting and HVAC firms, weights and measure specialists, printers and packagers as well as security and transportation service providers. It only makes sense that they seek out and put to use practices and processes from other related industries.

Most businesses have learned how to work with the rules and regulations provided by their state and local municipalities. These rules and regulations often vary from region to region and require companies to understand and implement process changes and controls that help the business meet those requirements in an efficient and cost-effective manner. For the most part, the cannabis industry continues to learn, grow and evolve.

The news cycle in the United States is rapid-fire and sensational. Bad press for one company is bad press for the industry. Businesses should be looking beyond their own interests and see themselves as part of the larger community forging new roads together, sharing knowledge, and answering the consumer safety questions in an articulate fashion with a singular industry voice.

The most important part of understanding the rules and regulations is realizing the needs and goals behind them. To be in compliance is certainly important and should be a goal for every cannabis company. Rules, regulations, and oversight are put into effect to protect consumers and are in place for good reason.

The United States is a consumer-driven society. This mass consumerism is due in large part to regulations. People walk into restaurants and grocery stores millions of times per day and don't even think twice about eating the food they purchase. People buy cars; travel on planes and trains; take prescription medications – all without thinking about what goes into the process that ensures their safety. As a society, the U.S. citizens place a great deal of 'blind trust' in regulatory oversight.

Make no mistake and don't overlook the fact that the newly forming cannabis industry is the recipient and beneficiary of years of consumerism and regulation. When cannabis consumers walk into a recreational store or dispensary, they (usually) don't ask for a tour, request to see the analytical reports, and grower backgrounds on who's supplying the product. They trust the store owner is running their business according to proper health standards, rules, and regulations.

All U.S. industries have rules and regulations to adhere to. It's up to the cannabis industry to maintain that trust by not only adhering to the state-by-state rules and regulations but going beyond regulatory expectations in light of the stringent scrutiny the industry is facing.

Striking the balance between good regulation and public safety is always a challenge between those tasked with oversight and the businesses struggling to be in compliance while maintaining a profit. The cannabis industry is no different. Businesses in every vertical market have learned how to create processes that meet or exceed regulatory requirements for safety and consumer satisfaction. Companies also hire quality assurance professionals and third-party auditing companies to make sure they are, at the very least, maintaining the minimum regulations.

Associations like Underwriters Laboratories (UL) for electronics, International Aviation Transport Association (IATA) for aviation, Good Manufacturing Practices for food and drugs, and American National Standards Institute (ANSI) for a myriad of other standards—further work to protect the public's safety.

These organizations are independent of government oversight but work within industries to create standards and best practices. To aid in these standards, even more, organizations exist like the International Standards Organization (ISO) and Global Standard Institute (GSI). These organizations exist to help businesses become better and more efficient at what they do.

In many cases, these processes have actually helped many companies improve profitability by increasing yields, lowering failures, reducing waste, and improving productivity. The most successful companies have embraced quality programs like Total Quality Management (TQM) and Six Sigma and thoroughly document these processes and procedures while auditing them continuously.

Many brands in the industry seem to be reactive to regulations rather than proactive. The cannabis industry is now at a point where introspection and a larger, global view are necessary. No one knows the industry better than the companies currently operating in it. And the understanding of what the industry needs to work on within itself is inherent in every business. Creating best practices and procedures for operation, beyond the basics of regulation, will benefit individual companies, and all of those yet to come. Very appropriately here, Benjamin Franklin wrote, "We must all hang together or assuredly we shall all hang separately."

## Cannabis Industry Associations

Industry organizations are critically important to these efforts. The Marijuana Policy Project, National Cannabis Industry Association, Cannabis Industry Group, Las Vegas Medical Cannabis Association, Colorado Cannabis Chamber of Commerce, and the International Cannabis Association are just a few of the different industry  organizations that businesses can join to affect positive change. These kinds of groups are perfectly situated to bring businesses together on issues like packaging, labeling, verbiage; and while founded or not, these subjects continue to fuel the news cycle. By addressing these issues within these organizations, sharing knowledge, and cozying up with state regulatory agencies, the individual brands can raise the bar for the industry as a whole.

It's also time for industry groups to move beyond advocacy. This does not diminish the need for advocacy, but it has become clear that with so many states adopting cannabis policies, advocacy groups have been extremely effective. These groups should now begin looking at efforts to protect the industry and guide businesses into best practices that not only protect consumers but also project the image the industry wants to be portrayed to the general public. These organizations can also take leadership roles with the special interest groups with the greatest concerns.

Each business, regardless of size, can bring value to the table. Creating awareness campaigns that make commitments to address relevant issues show the general public a commitment to safety. Creating standards around labeling, packaging, testing, communication and public education in cooperation with regulators also show our industry's desire to change current perceptions. Creating industry association standards encourage best practices and reward companies that step up to the challenge.

The cannabis industry has been effective and has kept its momentum. It is now in the hands of the same industry and each and every business within it to determine how to proceed and where to best focus. Will the industry be viewed as responsible, ethical, and forward-looking – or – reckless and unconcerned with public safety and its own image? I am confident, it's the former as examples below clearly show how canna-brands have been proactive in utilizing child-resistant packaging and are most certainly concerned about their products and the safety of the general public.

## Cannabis Brands Use Child-Resistant Packacing in New Ways

Henri Breault, the Canadian Director of Poison Control was instrumental in the creation of the first child-resistant container. He established the Association for the Control of Accidental Poisoning in 1962 and enabled the 1967 invention of a cap design known as the "Palm N Turn"—which has since become the standard in child-resistant packaging.

"Palm N Turn" Child Resistant Cap Invented in 1967 by Canadian Doctor Henri Breault

Although Child-Resistant (CR) packaging is part of everyday life, poisoning still remains a hazard to children. In 2014, the American Association of Poison Control Centers received about three million calls from consumers for poison exposure treatment or information and poisoning still causes about 30 pediatric deaths each year.[1]

CR packaging is required by regulation for prescription drugs, over-the-counter medications, pesticides, and household chemicals. In some jurisdictions, unit packaging such as blister packs is also regulated to ensure child safety.

Cheeba Chews Child Resistant Blister Pack

## The Need For Evolution

Although CR packaging is well established, new CR designs are being sought. It's likely several forces are responsible for this growing attention:

- Additions to the list of products requiring CR packaging
- The legalization of medical/recreational cannabis use in several states
- Widespread publicity about poisoning incidents related to detergent "pods"
- An ongoing shift from rigid containers to flexible packaging

In fact, the number of CR options for flexible packaging is expanding. The Presto Child-Guard slider zipper from Reynolds Presto Products Co. unzips the pouch when the slider tongue is aligned with a groove, depressed, and pulled. PPi Technologies uses this re-closable CR zipper for its Canna-PaQ™ standup pouch for cannabis. The CannaPaQ™ line also includes a pouch equipped with a large orifice fitment and CR closure.

Child-Resistant CannaPaQ™ Standup Pouch by PPi Technologies

## Tragic Numbers

Every 30 seconds in both the United States and Europe, an accidental poisoning is reported. More than 800,000 children are rushed to a hospital with symptoms of poisoning. Of these, 100,000 are actually hospitalized. In Europe alone, 3,000 young children die each year from the consequences of accidental poisoning by medicines or poisoning due to the ingestion of household chemicals. Children five years and under account for the majority of all poisoning accidents.[2]

> "More than 90% of all poisonings occur within the home environment and many common household products can poison children, including cleaning supplies, alcohol, plants, pesticides, medicine, and cosmetics."
> - United States Consumer Product Safety Commission

When selecting packaging materials and components for solid oral drugs, drug manufacturers and now cannabis processors must balance the needs of both children and adults. Charged under the Poison Prevention

Packaging Act of 1970 to design packages that help protect children from potentially toxic drugs, manufacturers must also make sure that adults who have limited dexterity can use the packages properly. Devising such a package isn't always a scientific endeavor, because manufacturers must base their selections on unpredictable factors like marketplace opinions and child testers. Add to this mix the expectations of the United States Consumer Product Safety Commission (CPSC), which hopes to eliminate child poisonings through regulation but offers manufacturers little guidance in package selection.

## CREATIVE COMPLIANCE

Proper cannabis labeling and packaging is a crucial component to staying in compliance with state guidelines. Cannabis companies must ensure that their packages are tamper-proof, child-resistant, and in accordance with their local laws. Businesses are forced to keep up with the perpetual tweaks being made to comply with changing regulations assuring the safety and security of the general public.

Child Resistant Box by
Locked4Kids

Designers of child-resistant packaging must always work against the paradox that a package difficult for a child to open, can often also be difficult for the adult patient it is intended to treat. In fact, up to 90 percent of adults struggle to open child-resistant packaging, according to a report in the Journal Of The Engineering And Physical Sciences Research Council.[3]

While there's no consistent—one set of rules and guidelines—for cannabis packaging across states where it is medically and recreationally legal, there are resources available to help maintain the brand's look and feel—while following state rules and requirements.

*"We're attentive to the structural aspects and required safety features of the package—while never losing sight of the brand's essence. We've had some great experiences and early success in the cannabis sector and project more of the same as we further develop our industry relationships."*

*- Nancy Gruskin Warner, Founder, Assurpack*

Assurpack, Locked4Kids, and CoolJarz are but just a few of the firms that have formed to assist cannabis brand owners to work through the ins and outs of child-resistant packaging in-line with varying state rules and regulations. Brands often find more stringent rules imposed by their city and county than their states. Further, Washington and Colorado's recreational packaging laws also vary greatly—causing 'mass customization' across state lines as brands grow nationally.

A solid example of this is the Dixie brand. Working closely with a pharmaceutical and consumer product packaging industry expert, Dixie leveraged years of experience to create child-resistant packaging for their "Toasted Rooster" and "Crispy Kraken" chocolate bars.

Dixie's Child-Resistant Packaged "Toasted Rooster" Chocolate Bar

---

*"We've found a multi-state child-resistant solution for our chocolate and mint products while remaining true to the Dixie brand"*

- LINDSEY TOPPING, DIXIE'S DIRECTOR OF MARKETING

---

It's in the industry's best interest not to reinvent the wheel, but rather borrow and implement existing best practices from relevant sectors such as pharmaceuticals, cosmetics, and other consumer packaged goods products. There is no doubt those brands that can maintain products in-line with state-to-state regulations and stay true to their brand essence will rise above.

It's on cannabis brands to create safe, consistent products in the safest child-resistant packages available. It's on the CPSC to do a better job of educating people on how to use child-resistant packaging and why it's important to put it away after use—even though it's considered child-resistant. Together as an industry, we can protect our children if we are assertive about teaching adults to properly use child-resistant packages. Bottom line: No package is 100 percent safe for cannabis nor any other prescribed or adult consumable.

## IT'S NOT EASY BEING GREEN

The recent health movement and the mindset fueling it have changed the way we eat and think about our food and our food chain. Organic, non-GMO, gluten-free, and pesticide-free are trends that affect our eating habits as well as our health and wellbeing.

Similarly, within the cannabis sector, many producers are working toward creating healthier products. Some are acting upon their desire to produce healthier products in-line with their brand promise. Others see consumer demand for healthier products and are responding to it, and some continue to use approved pesticides according to state rules and regulations.

Examples of recent "health-conscious" trends in the cannabis sector - some now being called out on packaging as product benefits and/or attributes include the move away from using food-grade Polyethylene glycol (PEG) to cut cannabis oil for vaporizing—and toward using natural hemp and/or coconut oil instead. Another trend includes the move away from traditional flavors such as cherry, watermelon, and other fruit flavors—which appeal to children—and toward reintroducing natural terpenes such as myrcene, limonene, pinene, etc.

> *"Today, the honor system is being used in the pseudo-regulated market. Randomized pesticide testing should be added to the current testing portfolio, and cannabis companies should be fully transparent about what ingredients and additives they use in their products. The more transparent, the better."*
>
> *- TOBIAS COUGHLIN-BOGUE, THE STRANGER*

Accordingly, the concept of growth for production while reducing and eliminating pesticide use through beneficial insects and nematodes, microbial products, pest management tools like traps and lures, just to name a few are on the rise. Other examples of the move toward "healthier" cannabis products include a number of organic certifications.' Legally, cannabis cannot be called 'organic'—no matter how environmentally friendly the cultivation practices remain. The term 'organic' is federally regulated and the USDA does not recognize cannabis as a legitimate agricultural crop. Further, the Environmental Protection Agency won't test pesticides used on cannabis while it's considered a Schedule I drug.

> *"A lot of research goes into pesticide allowance and pesticide labeling for agricultural crops, but because cannabis is federally illegal, and is smoked, not ingested, there is little comparable research relating to human health effects."*
>
> *- JESSICA CORCORRAN, SOUND HORTICULTURE*

As crop supply chains lengthen, it becomes increasingly more difficult for consumers to "know their grower." Without a connection to the producer, how does a consumer know which products are grown using chemical fertilizers and/or toxic pesticides?

Clean Green™ and Certified Kind™—both organic cannabis certifications—are influenced by global organic standards. They draw upon the principles of organic production articulated by the International Federation of Organic Agricultural Movements (IFOAM) and are similar to the organic regulations of the United States, Canada, the European Union, and Mexico. Much like the USDA National Organic Program for traditional agricultural products, the whole life cycle of the plant is considered, from seed selection to harvesting and processing, as well as soil, nutrients, pesticide use, mold treatment, and dust control.

## Inhalation Of Pesticides Residues

More broadly, some see complications related to pesticides as normal for a young industry. Very little peer-reviewed research has been published on the health and safety risks associated with pesticides on dried cannabis. However, tests that have been performed show cause for significant consumer concern, particularly with medical patients or those with elevated risk factors.

Authors of the Journal of Toxicology Study[4] note that "High pesticide exposure through cannabis smoking is a significant possibility, which may lead to further health complications in cannabis users." Other concerns surround the concentrated higher levels of pesticides in extracted oils. Still, a concern that pesticides could upset the balance between the industry and the federal government lingers.

> *"We have an incubated environment we're allowed to operate in right now. If we open up opportunities for people to use dangerous things on plants, it becomes an embarrassment and we invite more scrutiny. It would be a huge step backward."*
> - DEREK PETERSON, CEO, TERRA TECH

The Pesticide Information Center Online[5] database lists all the pesticides that are allowed on cannabis in Washington State is freely available on the Washington State University website.

*"There has been no actual testing to verify that the final cannabis consumable does not contain any pesticide residue. In fact, until recently there were no labs able to perform cannabis pesticide testing, which of course kept the public unaware that our cannabis contains pesticides."*

— MURACO KYASHNA-TOCHA, CANNABIS SAFETY ACTIVIST

Due to the Washington State Department of Health's proposed rules for "compliant" products, including requirements for pesticide residue testing, Washington State's labs have been gearing up to offer such services in order to meet the state's July 1, 2016 deadline for retailers to begin offering compliant products to medical patients.

Some pesticide products are systemic; meaning a certain degree of the chemicals will remain with the plant throughout its life and will exist in clone cuttings of these plants too. Even though this is the case, the Washington State Liquor and Cannabis Board does not make any allowances for this, citing any pesticide presence more than zero percent as being contaminated.[6]

The Environmental Protection Agency has reported almost one billion pounds of pesticide used annually for agricultural use. Unlike our food products though, cannabis is usually inhaled, not consumed, and broken down by our digestive system.

Since cannabis is typically inhaled, Washington State lawmakers want to ensure that there are no serious impacts on the lungs or respiratory system. That said, as long as cannabis is considered and classified as a Schedule I drug, there will be limited data regarding pesticides and their effects on cannabis consumers.

## Understanding Consumer Trends Through Data

Particularly on the manufacturing and retail front, understanding the composition of the average cannabis consumer's purchase is incredibly important. Understanding the composition of purchases also yields insights as to when customers buy the most and which category(ies) they buy at which times or in which combinations. Better understanding customer activities and buying habits can help cannabis professionals use Key Performance Indicators (KPIs) to make informed decisions about product selection, merchandising, bundling, cross-promotion, and more.

Understanding what items tend to be bought together—eggs and bacon on Sunday morning, for example—helps retailers offer specials that resonate with their customers and organize their store in a way that drives sales and effectively connects consumers with the products they're seeking. It also offers useful information on pricing, loyalty programs, inventory, and marketing. Making effective use of this type of data helps brand owners and retailers compete more successfully in an increasingly competitive market by fine-tuning their marketing programs and inventory management to match the preferences and proclivities of their customer base.

## Summary

If it hasn't been made apparent enough, innovation and best practices allow us to employ methods, processes, and/or programs that have been tested and found to increase the chances that one will successfully accomplish their goals and objectives. There are, however, further reasons why the use of best practices can be advantageous.

- Using a recognized best practice makes it easier to justify the work. If an organization or initiative is starting from scratch, the community and especially potential participants may be justifiably skeptical. Demonstrating using a best practice that has been shown to be effective can relieve skepticism and help gain support.
- Using recognized best practices could bolster the credibility of an organization and brand; showing it not only is using a tested process but that it has been conducting research and assuring quality control.
- Using best practices can make it easier to get funding. Funders look more favorably on proposals that can demonstrate proven success and Key Performance Indicators (KPIs).
- Using a best practice removes a lot of the guesswork from planning. Employing a program or method whose structure and process are carefully documented makes it easier to implement and increases the probability of success.
- Most important, we know that best practices work. They've been shown to provide the changes in behavior or conditions and the outcomes we're interested in.

Leveraging systems and processes that help a brand monitor and increase its performance, will allow that brand to better compete and sustain brand innovation, loyalty, and trust in the long run.

## CHAPTER TEN

# THE FUTURE OF CANNABIS

---

*"The US has become the world reference in the legal production of cannabis. The short-term future in the worldwide industry will be based on the exportation of its innovative approach in terms of marketing and product. However, the market limitation for brands expanding beyond each state is resulting in a lack of recognition on an international level. Even the most prestigious brands at the State level are not recognizable in other countries. This recognition and exportation will need to be done through creative partnerships and new ways of production."*

— MIGUEL PELLON, FOUNDER, AMERICANNABIS

---

## A MID-PANDEMIC FORECAST

While few companies may one day emerge as the Starbucks, Marlboro, Pfizer, or Anheuser-Busch of cannabis, they have not yet arrived. That said, it's not a matter of if "big industry" will arrive, it's a matter of when.

Retail sales of medical marijuana (MMJ) and recreational cannabis will hit between $3.5 billion and $4.3 billion in 2016, which amounts to year-over-year growth of 17% to 26%, according to estimates in the Cannabis Business Factbook.[1] With a billion dollars in revenues expected in Colorado alone this year, large corporations will eventually follow the money and turn what is now merely a highly fragmented craft industry, into one where big companies rule and smaller players get weeded out.

When they do, the mom-and-pop shops that populate the cannabis space now will find it challenging to remain small and independent. That said, they would also have new opportunities to grow into larger companies, partner with big firms, and/or sell-out to the highest bidder.

Outwardly, tobacco giants and other large companies don't want to be seen making a move into an industry that is still out of favor in many circles – the opposite of where tobacco was heading - especially if cannabis is in some form decriminalized federally.

Tobacco companies vehemently denied interest in cannabis in the 1970s, when legalization appeared a possibility. But recently unearthed documents revealed that some of the largest players were indeed developing plans to enter the industry.

> *"Not everybody is convinced the cannabis industry is being sussed-out by tobacco companies. Instead, some believe that alcohol or pharmaceutical firms are more likely to move-in."*
>
> - ZACK HUTSON, PRIVATEER HOLDINGS

"We [Privateer Holdings] actually don't think that tobacco will be interested in the space the way alcohol or pharma might," Hutson said. "Tobacco companies are in the addiction business and that's not what cannabis is about."[2]

But even alcohol and pharmaceutical firms are reluctant to discuss the cannabis industry, let alone reveal any interest. Still, experts and those close to other industries say these companies are indeed exploring opportunities.

"That doesn't mean they will come in overnight. It will likely take the Federal Government decriminalizing cannabis before large corporations move into the space, as none are willing to put up with so much risk for, in relative terms, a marginal return," Hutson said.

Instead, it will be institutional investors such as Peter Thiel's Founders Fund that will move into the industry. As they do, Wall Street will take notice, analysts will begin covering the industry and larger corporations will arrive. "It's inevitable that a Fortune 500 company will move into the space, but it will take the end of the federal Prohibition before that happens," he continued.

So, what are the most relevant and pertinent reasons for this change?

## Money

The war on cannabis costs money. The direct costs to local, state, and federal governments are staggering and exceed a trillion dollars. Police, prosecutors, probation officers, judges, courts, jailers, prison guards, and defense lawyers form a massive prison-industrial complex that distracts limited resources away from our failing economy and other more import- ant priorities. The indirect costs to the economy, though more difficult to quantify, are probably higher in the form of people removed from their families and their jobs, the opportunity costs of distracted police, and jammed courts too busy to adjudicate important criminal and civil cases.[3]

## A Failed Drug War

The U.S. government continues to pour more lawyers, police, and money into the militarized cannabis Prohibition, yet people still easily obtain cannabis. In 2015, the number of people arrested in the U.S. for a canna- bis violation was 643,121. Of those arrested with cannabis law violations, 574,641 (89 percent) were arrested for possession only.[4]

## Freedom

The war on cannabis is alien to the principles of a free nation founded on the principles of limited government and personal responsibility. The negative impacts of cannabis Prohibition laws far outweigh the negative impact of the substance itself.

Humans in all cultures have used the cannabis plant since the dawn of history for medicinal, spiritual, industrial, and recreational purposes; only in the twentieth century did it occur to any government to prohibit it. Thomas Jefferson and other founders grew cannabis on their plantations. The Declaration Of Independence is written on hemp paper.

The history of American cannabis Prohibition and "reefer madness" shows that its practical and legal basis is a house of cards. An outgrowth of alcohol Prohibition that arose in roughly the same era, cannabis Prohibition was born out of racially charged fears of Mexicans and African Americans.[5]

## Saftey

The war on cannabis, like alcohol Prohibition before it, creates and fuels the criminal underclass, organized crime, and domestic and foreign drug cartels. It is basic economics: where there is a demand, a supply will be created to meet it, period. Human demand for cannabis, like alcohol, has lasted thousands of years, and will never go away. Leading economists like Milton Friedman have long seen the drug war as an economically bankrupt policy.

If cannabis were legalized and taxed, violent drug cartels would lose the principal source of their income. Cannabis ought to be treated like alcohol, available at the corner store, taxed, and regulated. How many drug cartels smuggle beer over the border?

## Children

Often, it is easier for American children to obtain cannabis than beer. That is because the government has created a black market for cannabis, making it more accessible to children. There is no black market for beer. It is relatively cheap and easy to obtain, for adults, but difficult for children.

For these reasons and more, Americans have now passed the critical 50 percent threshold in support of cannabis legalization.

Some say legalization is immoral. Perhaps if they believe there's a principled basis for discriminating against people based solely on what they consume—absent of harm to others—then they may have grounds for an argument. Others say legalization would open the floodgates to huge increases in drug use and create a "marijuana nation." Perhaps the greatest possible downside to legalization may be that the legal market(s) fall into the hands of alcohol, tobacco, and pharmaceutical companies.

> *"Successful canna-businesses are building brands, based on community values, patient and consumer benefits, and competitive advantages. Regrettably, due to federal prohibition and the resulting patchwork of state laws, brand name collision is looming—as local, state, and national brands expand. Incorporating marijuana memes and slang in a brand name or adopting a ubiquitous or laudatory designation raises the potential for conflict because those terms have a greater likelihood of having been already adopted or registered elsewhere."*
>
> - MARY SHAPIRO, ESQ., EVOKE LAW

Harvard University economist Dr. Jeffrey Miron has written a study entitled "The Budgetary Implications of Cannabis Prohibition"[6] endorsed by over 500 economists including Nobel Prize-winner Milton Friedman. In his paper, Miron concludes that instituting legal regulations will save the government $7.7 billion just by not having to enforce current prohibition laws ($2.4 billion at the federal level and $5.3 billion at the state and local levels). He goes on to state that tax revenue could range from $2.4 billion per year if cannabis were taxed like ordinary consumer goods to $6.2 billion if it were more heavily taxed like alcohol or tobacco.[7]

The legal cannabis industry in the U.S. may grow to $50 billion in the next decade, expanding to more than eight times its current size, as lawful pot purveyors gain new customers and win over users from the illicit market, according to a new report by research firm Cowen & Co.[8] The legalization of recreational use in California, where the drug is already medically permitted, alone tripled the size of the nation's current $6 billion legal industry, according to a report from Cowen & Co.

The expanding industry will affect big business even though the current competitive landscape is largely made up of smaller startups. Because cannabis is federally illegal, large companies have shied away from getting involved. This will change once the federal laws and scheduling change.

Tobacco companies may make up about one-fifth of the cannabis industry by 2036, adding more than 20 percent to their revenue, and nearly doubling tobacco's underlying growth, analysts said. Vapor technology – a popular technique for ingesting both tobacco and cannabis – is an essential part of big tobacco's less combustible-dependent future. Companies like Altria Group Inc. and Reynolds American Inc. already have expertise in vapor and crop-growing technologies, as well as familiarity dealing with complex regulatory frameworks.[9]

For both potential winners and losers, the scale of the predicted changes is unusual, analysts suggest. "A 24 percent, 10-year revenue compound annual growth rate is hard to find in consumer staples. In particular, one with a $50-plus billion endpoint," Cowen analysts reveal.[10]

"Legalization" is a big concept with many different models. There has truly never been a more exciting time in history for cannabis than the present. We are in some ways, loving the dream and fighting for it. From a reform and business perspective, the future looks bright even as we await the President-Elect's perspective on cannabis reform and/or legalization. Rest assured, there will be hurdles. Hurdles due to the stigmas that exist including Schedule I categorization, tax laws, banking systems, and interstate commerce issues –to name a few.

We will see attempts by the alcohol, tobacco, and pharmaceutical industries to enter the cannabis space. While their entrance might not initially be successful (as 'core' consumers prefer purchasing their cannabis products from local growers), it's just a matter of time before new or casual consumers find their way to those products that are positioned and packaged as consistent consumable goods – something the larger industries are experts at.

Moving forward, we'll see a heavier influence from women than any other industry of comparable size. There are so many talented women in the cannabis industry. More and more will find new careers in the future and they will thrive. Organizations like Women Grow will help empower women to find their place within the industry.

Form factors will continue to develop and evolve on the medical, recreational, and therapeutic fronts. There will always be those that smoke and those that can't or prefer not to. Accordingly, new means and methods of consistently controlling and discretely dosing will continue to be explored.

> *"One very welcome trend is a move away from engineering-driven concepts towards idea driven concepts that cater to today's cannabis consumer. As an example, instead of silly strain names that give pause to prohibitionists, you'll soon see "Sunday Brunch" type strain names that explore a sought-after vibe or feeling that crosses so many demographics."*
>
> *- LESLIE BOCSKOR, FOUNDER, ELECTRUM PARTNERS*

The near future will see more cannabis research conducted and more discoveries made. Research being conducted in Israel, the U.K., and other countries are very promising as it relates to the plant's efficacy and benefits.

From a pure industry growth perspective, there's no reason to doubt that there will be significant growth on many fronts. Ranging from manufacturing and production including real estate, soil, fertilizer, and lights through child-resistant packaging and machinery to enclose cannabis and cannabis-infused products. Banking, security, and financial services will continue to develop and prosper as laws change across states and at the federal level. Cannabis classes, education, and trade schools will become the norm. Accredited universities will offer cannabis courses as well as the emergence of industry associations, summits, seminars, and expos.

We already see cannabis consumers targeted as a 'social demographic.' Jack In The Box's obvious cannabis insinuations and Wonderful Pistachios commercials leveraging Snoop Dogg using 'insider' cannabis jargon is evidence of this phenomenon. The U.S. cannabis consumer market is made up of tens of millions of consumers. Snack food manufacturers to eye whitening brands will be soon marketing to the cannabis consumer.

Over time, we will see the normalization of cannabis and cannabis consumption. It will eventually be perceived as just another consumer product good. Whether medical, recreational, or therapeutic, cannabis will be considered as mainstream as any plant, fruit, or vegetable. The biases, stereotypes, and snarky puns will be a thing of the past. Wall Street firms will hire cannabis analysts. Media outlets will hire cannabis correspondents. Cannabis companies will hire lobbyists. And eventually, we will come full circle to a day where canna-brands too, will advertise like the big pharmaceutical companies we see today stating, "Ask your doctor if it's right for you." It's inevitable.

"Legal cannabis has gone from grassroots cottage industry to global big business in less than a decade. The industry which initially fought to establish its viability and legitimacy, has quickly gone mainstream. Rather than one industry, legal cannabis in some form is now a part of almost every industry–the spectrum of legal products ranges from medicines to health and beauty aids, from fuels and fibers to fabrics and foods; consumables to cars, pet foods to biodegradable plastics, legal cannabis is disrupting and reinvigorating the way the world does business, replacing the petrochemical economy that has been in place since World War I."

- DAVID RHEINS, FOUNDER AND EXECUTIVE DIRECTOR, MJBA

## CONCLUSION

Onward and upward. As an advocate for the legalization (and sensible regulation) of cannabis, there has been no better time and place than to have spent the last ten years in Seattle. Through the course of writing this book, I have been fortunate enough to travel, meet and interview hundreds of cannabis industry influencers both within and outside of the United States. From my time spent with producers and processors, investors, brand owners, entrepreneurs, IP attorneys, cannabis media, dispensary owners, and recreational retailers—I have learned more than I ever anticipated. In fact, I've witnessed the rise of a newly formed industry playing a formidable role in the legalization of cannabis around the world.

It's time we see the puritanical perspective imposed by the Nixon Administration, their successors, and the scorched earth trail they created, a thing of the past. It's time to move forward together raising the collective bar, acting as stewards of the industry—guiding and educating the uninformed on the benefits of cannabis and its components.

Today, more than 1.5 million Americans are incarcerated in state and federal prisons, a figure that has quintupled since 1980. Adding in jails, the number of Americans who are behind bars rises to 2.2 million. One in three U.S. adults has been arrested by age 23—many for small amounts of cannabis possession. Communities of color are disproportionately affected. As a result, between 70 million and 100 million—or as many as one in three Americans—have some type of criminal record. Having even a minor criminal record, such as a misdemeanor or even an arrest without conviction, can create an array of lifelong barriers that stand in the way of successful re-entry. This has broad implications for individuals' and families' economic security, as well as for our national economy. Mass incarceration and hyper-criminalization serve as major drivers of poverty; having a criminal record can present obstacles to employment, housing, public assistance, education, family reunification, building good credit, and more.[11]

The extreme injustice of building a new legal industry that prospers off a plant that has incarcerated so many people, especially in communities of color must be recognized. We must set a place at the table for them and let them share in the "industry" that's taking shape. It's a privilege to witness and participate in the development, but it's also a responsibility to step up and work towards change. Thankfully, the stigma caused by 80+ years of criminalization is changing and is reflected by shifting regulations and more people taking an interest in the plant's benefits; but these do not equate to reparations for the damage inflicted onto marginalized communities. Now is not the time for "virtue signaling," but rather building an equitable cannabis industry that repairs its past while creating its future.

As we live through the COVID-19 pandemic and current social unrest, there are lessons to be learned every day. In many ways, we've been turned upside down. Schools, places of business, and houses of worship have been closed—while cannabis dispensaries have been deemed "essential." Indeed, it's time for a new awakening. A new reality where we collectively engage in equity, justice, inclusion, and accountability.

If we let her, cannabis can help us rebuild our post-pandemic economy, as well as heal our bodies and minds. Legalized at the federal level, a regulated, national cannabis industry would create jobs, generate tax revenue, and increase economic benefit across many sectors including agriculture, manufacturing, technology, packaging, retail, direct-to-consumer, among others. It's time we let her heal us from the inside out and the outside in.

---

*"It is in my humble opinion that the leading trend to long-term success in the cannabis industry is a true passion and respect for the plant. With that, one is able to not only time and time again ride the rollercoaster of the industry, but also innovate and lead while being successful."*

- ALEX COOLEY, SOLSTICE, CO-FOUNDER

---

# ACKNOWLEDGEMENTS

## A Very Special Thanks To:

Aaron Ball, Aaron Bios, Aaron Pelley, Aaron Silverman, Aaron Varney, Abraham Krongold, Adam Dunn, Adam Levin, Adam Schatz, Adam Smith, Ah Warner, Alan Brochstein, CFA, Alex Cooley, Alexander K Harris, Allie Beckett, Alyssa Anderson, Amanda Fish, Andrea Larson, Andrew Floor, Andrew Oldfield, Andrew Sorkin, Andy Bright, Andy Williams, Anne Raynor, Anthony Davis, Anna Shreeve, April Pride, Ariel Payopay, Benjamin Paleschuck₁, Benjamin Paleschuck₂, Berrin Noorata, Billi Kid, Bill Fickett, Brad Douglass, Brandon David, Brandon Lanich, Brandy A. Babin, Brendan Kennedy, Brett Gellein, Brian Orange, Brian Wansolich, Brianna Hughes, Bruce Castillo, Bruce Milligan, Bruce Mirken, Bryce Nichter, Bryan Suter, Cameron Harris, Candice Owens, Celeste Miranda, Charlie Cassidy, Cheryl Shuman, Cheyenne Fowler, Chris Galvin, Chris Walsh, Christian Hageseth, Christina Heintzelman, Christopher Male, Christy Quinto, Chuck Bredl, Cy Scott, Dale Sky Jones, Dan Zuckerman, Daniel Philipp, Danny Danko, Dorota Umeno, Dave Carpenter, Dave Inman, Dave Mesford, David Tran, Dax Colwell, Derek McCarty, Derek Petersen, Derek Vanderwarker, Douglas Moore, Dr. Lakisha Jenkins, Drake Sutton-Shearer, Durban Poison, Ed Rosenthal, Eighth Day Create, Eileen Nammanny, Eli Sanders, Elizabeth Hogan, Emily Resling, Eric Erlandsen, Eric Gaston, Eric Layland, Eric Ogden, Erik Hecht, Evan Carter, Evan Eneman, Evan Nison, Evan Senn, Gabe Fertman, Gavin Kogan, George Elder, Gia Garganese, Glace Bondeson, Graham Sorkin, Greg Warme, Gussie Paleschuck, Guy Barudin, Hayley Fickett, Hezekiah Blake, Ian Eisenberg, Imelda Walavalkar, James DeRose, James Zachodni, Jamie Hoffman, Jane Klein, Jane Petit, Jared Mirsky, Jason Pinsky, Jason Warden, Jeff Jones, Jeff Raber, Jeffrey Friedland, Jeffrey Rosen, Jena Schlosser, Jerry Rubin, Jessa Lewis, Jessica Corcorran, Jessica Lee, Jhavid Mohseni, Jigga, Jody Hall, Joe Dolce, Joe Paleschuck, John Arbour, John Dunwoody, John Welsh, Johnnie Walker, Jonathan Teeters, JonPaul Woodliff, Jorge Hermida, Josh Kirby, Joshua Berman, Joshua Otten, Joy Contreras, Jupiter

Hotel, Juse Barros, Justin Jones, Karina Masolova, Kate Quackenbush, Kayli Nugent, Kemi Adeyemi, Ken Loritz, Ken Loo, Kenny Morrison, Kory Kirby, Kristi Knoblich, Krystal Estrada, Lannie Lafreniere, Larry Perrigo, Leslie Bocskor, Lenny Gaiter, Linda Kepper, Lindsay Gatz, Lindsay Topping, Madeline Donegan, Marco Hoffman, Maria Moses, Mark Coffin, Mark McGrath, Mark Pettinger, Marni Fechter, Mary Shapiro, Esq., Mathew Anderson, Matthew Reus, Maurice Paleschuck, Michael Blatter, Michael Blunk, Michael Esshaki, Michael Hurt, Michelle Glassman, Miguel Pellón, Mike Appezzato, Mike Basilicato, Mike Garganese, Mike Genovese, Miq Willmott, Monah Zhang, Mr. T, Mrs. T, Mustafa "Moose" Filiz, Nancy Warner, Nate Gibbs, Nathan T. Paine, NATIV Hotel, Nelson Miyazaki, Nick Berchtold, Nick Grappone, Nick Jikomes, Nico Trehearne, Nicole Smith, Nisa Trehearne, Noel Remigio, NYC Diesel, Ophelia Chong, Oscar Velasco-Schmitz, Pamela Johnston, Patrick Scanlon, Paul Amsbury, Paul Caffrey, Pearl Paleschuck, Rachel Bussey, Richard Hebbourn, Rick "Ranger" Stevens, Rick "Rude Operator" Reams, Rita Tasmajian, Rosie Wright, Sage Mary James, Sally Vander Veer, Salwa Ibrahim, Sandra Semling, Sanjay Gupta, Sarah Holyhead, Sarah Krongold, Sarah Sandoval, Saul Kaye, Scott Berman, Scott Dittman, Scott Vickers, Shanel Lindsay, Esq, Shanon Melick, Sherbinski, Shmuel Tennenhaus, Stacy Benjamin, Stephanie Wright, Steph Sherer, Steve Miller, Steven Marshank, Tahira Rehmatullah, Tangie, Tim Strombel, Tobias Coughlin-Bogue, Toby Skard, Tom Gregory, Tom Hymes, Tonya Reilly, Tracy Anderson, Travis Lachner, Trek Manzoni, Trevor Gallup, Will Denman, Zachary Holland, Zack Hutson and Zoe Huden.

# REFERENCES

## INTRODUCTION

1 "Cannabinoid Dose and Label Accuracy in Edible Medical Cannabis Products", The Journal of American Medicine (JAMA), June 2015; https://jamanetwork.com/journals/jama/fullarticle/2338239

2 Federal Government's 2013 Cole Memorandum; https://www.justice.gov/iso/opa/resources/3052013829132756857467.pdf

## CHAPTER 1

1 Half of Americans Continue to Support Legalizing Recreational Marijuana, 2015 Harris Poll; https://theharrispoll.com/as-of-last-months-elections-four-more-states-voted-to-decriminalize-marijuana-for-both-medical-and-recreational-use-bringing-the-grand-total-to-8-states-that-have-legalized-recreational-mar/

2 NORML: Half of Americans Continue to Support Legalizing Recreational Marijuana, 2015 Harris Poll; https://blog.norml.org/2018/07/30/harris-poll-majority-of-americans-want-marijuana-legalized/

3 Majority in U.S. Support Medical Pot, Think It Could Fight Opioid Crisis; https://theharrispoll.com/majority-in-u-s-support-medical-pot-think-it-could-fight-opioid-crisis/

4 Gallup: "Support For Marijuana Legalization Surges To New Highs"; https://www.washingtonpost.com/news/wonk/wp/2016/10/19/gallup-support-for-marijuana-legalization-surges-to-new-highs/?noredirect=on&utm_term=.bcdbba0a4e54

5 Gallup Poll, "Poll: Colorado still shows strong support for marijuana legalization"; http://www.thecannabist.co/2015/02/24/marijuana-legalization-poll-colorado/30346/

6 Gieringer 2002; "The Acceptance of Medicinal Marijuana in the U.S."; https://www.tandfonline.com/doi/abs/10.1300/J175v03n01_03

## CHAPTER 2

1 "University Of Saskatchewan Research Suggests Marijuana Analogue Stimulates Brain Cell Growth"; https://www.sciencedaily.com/releases/2005/10/051016083817.htm

2 Meet Anandamide - The "Bliss" Molecule; https://www.labroots.com/trending/cannabis-sciences/13150/meet-anandamide-bliss-molecule

3 "Why I Changed My Mind On Weed"; Dr. Sanjay Gupta, CNN Chief Medical Correspondent; https://www.cnn.com/2013/08/08/health/gupta-changed-mind-marijuana/index.html

4 "Rand Paul Courts Donors From Marijuana Industry"; https://www.cbsnews.com/news/election-2016-rand-paul-courts-donors-from-marijuana-pot-industry/

5 "Essential Oil Of Cannabis Sativa L. Strains; http://www.internationalhempassociation.org/jiha/jiha4208.html

## CHAPTER 3

1 "Hemp Can Save The World"; http://thelills.com/hemp-can-save-the-world/

2 "Uses of Hemp"; https://www.mit.edu/~thistle/v13/2/history.html

3 "The Prohibition of Marijuana"; https://beyondthc.com/the-prohibition-of-marijuana-2/

4 "The Genesis Of Marijuana Prohibition"; ttp://www.druglibrary.org/schaffer/Library/studies/vlr/vlr2.htm

5 "The Federal Marijuana Ban Is Rooted in Myth and Xenophobia"; https://www.nytimes.com/2014/07/30/opinion/high-time-federal-marijuana-ban-is-rooted-in-myth.html

6 "Marijuana - The First Twelve Thousand Years"; http://druglibrary.org/schaffer/hemp/history/first12000/12.htm

7 "Marijuana Prohibition Was Racist From The Start. Not Much Has Changed"; https://www.huffpost.com/entry/marijuana-prohibition-racist_n_4590190

8 "The Racist Roots of Marijuana Prohibition"; https://fee.org/articles/the-racist-roots-of-marijuana-prohibition/

9 "The Racist Roots of Marijuana Prohibition"; https://fee.org/articles/the-racist-roots-of-marijuana-prohibition/

## CHAPTER 4

1 "Hemp Makes a Return to George Washington's Farm"; https://www.smithsonianmag.com/smart-news/hemp-makes-return-george-washingtons-farm-180970131/

2 "The Cosmopolitan Lyceum: Lecture Culture and the Globe in Nineteenth-Century America": https://www.academia.edu/5684750/The_Cosmopolitan_Lyceum_Lecture_Culture_and_the_Globe_in_Nineteenth-Century_America

3 Some Of My Finest Hours Have Been Spent On My Back Veranda, Smoking Hemp … (Spurious Quotation)"; https://www.monticello.org/site/research-and-collections/some-my-finest-hours-have-been-spent-my-back-veranda-smoking-hemp

4 "A History Of Hemp" By Robert A. Nelson; http://www.rexresearch.com/hhist/hhist2.htm

5 "Pro-Pot Presidents"; https://www.softsecrets.com/us/news/national/pro-pot-presidents/

6 "Once and for all - which presidents got stoned?"; https://www.dailykos.com/stories/2014/8/25/1324564/-Once-and-for-all-which-presidents-got-stoned

7 "The U.S. Army And Irregular Warfare, 1775–2007"; http://www.baltdefcol.org/files/files/documents/Research/Books/Sibul%20-%20The%20US%20Army%20and%20Irregular%20Warfare.pdf

8 "The Very Important Blog"; https://www.veryimportantpotheads.com/blog2006.html

9 "Jimmy Carter says marijuana legalization is A-OK"; http://www.msnbc.com/the-last-word/jimmy-carter-says-marijuana-legalization

10 "Barack Obama, Asked About Drug History, Admits He Inhaled"; https://www.nytimes.com/2006/10/24/world/americas/24iht-dems.3272493.html

11 "Higher And Higher: American Drug Use In Vietnam"; http://nintharticle.com/vietnam-drug-usage.htm

12 "A Case Against Marijuana"; https://www.nytimes.com/2018/07/20/opinion/marijuana-legalization-colorado-health.html

13 "What Science Says About Marijuana"; https://www.nytimes.com/2014/07/31/opinion/what-science-says-about-marijuana.html

14 "Why I Changed My Mind On Weed" By Dr. Sanjay Gupta; https://www.cnn.com/2013/08/08/health/gupta-changed-mind-marijuana/index.html

## CHAPTER 5

1 "What are the Most Popular Cannabis Products?", Headset Report, June 29, 2016; https://www.headset. io/blog/what-are-the-most-popular-cannabis-products

2 "Who's Buying All That Pot? A Look at the Demographics of Cannabis Consumers 2017", October 6, 2017; https://www.headset.io/blog/whos-buying-all-that-pot-a-look-at-the-demographics-of-cannabis-consumers-2017

3 "What Does the Average Cannabis Consumer Look Like?", Headset Report, July 21, 2016; https://www.headset.io/blog/what-does-the-average-cannabis-consumer-look-like

4 "What Does the Average Cannabis Consumer Look Like?", Headset Report, July 21, 2016; https://www.headset.io/blog/what-does-the-average-cannabis-consumer-look-like

5 "What Does the Average Cannabis Consumer Look Like?", Headset Report, July 21, 2016; https://www.headset.io/blog/what-does-the-average-cannabis-consumer-look-like

6 "What Does the Average Cannabis Consumer Look Like?", Headset Report, July 21, 2016; https://www.headset.io/blog/what-does-the-average-cannabis-consumer-look-like

7 "What Does the Average Cannabis Consumer Look Like?", Headset Report, July 21, 2016; https://www.headset.io/blog/what-does-the-average-cannabis-consumer-look-like

8 "Basket Analysis Report", Headset Report, September 20, 2016; https://www.headset.io/blog/basket-analysis-report

9 "Vapor Pens: The Next Big Thing in Cannabis?", Headset Report, August 11, 2016; https://www.headset. io/blog/vapor-pens-the-next-big-thing-in-cannabis

10 "Product Co-Occurence: Impulse Buying and Upselling in the Cannabis Industry", Headset Report, February 28, 2017; https://www.headset.io/blog/product-co-occurence-impulse-buying-and-upselling-in-the-cannabis-industry

11 "What Does the Average Cannabis Consumer Look Like?", Headset Report, July 21, 2016; https://www.headset.io/blog/what-does-the-average-cannabis-consumer-look-like

12 "Cannabis Brand Study 2017 – Part 1", The Matters Group, 2017; https://canna-ventures.com/product/cannabis-brands-study-v2017/

13 "Cannabis Brand Study 2017 – Part 1", The Matters Group, 2017; https://canna-ventures.com/product/cannabis-brands-study-v2017/

14 "Cannabis Brand Study 2017 – Part 1", The Matters Group, 2017; https://canna-ventures.com/product/cannabis-brands-study-v2017/

15 "Cannabis Brand Study 2017 – Part 1", The Matters Group, 2017; https://canna-ventures.com/product/cannabis-brands-study-v2017/

16 "Cannabis Brand Study 2017 – Part 1", The Matters Group, 2017; https://canna-ventures.com/product/cannabis-brands-study-v2017/

17 "Cannabis Brand Study 2017 – Part 2", The Matters Group, 2017; https://canna-ventures.com/resources/cannabis-brand-research-summary-2/

18 "Cannabis Branding for Men & Women", The Matters Group, 2017; https://canna-ventures.com/resources/men-women-brand-research-white-paper/

19 "Cannabis Brand Study 2017 – Part 2", The Matters Group, 2017; https://canna-ventures.com/resources/cannabis-brand-research-summary-2/

20 "Cannabis Brand Study 2017 – Part 2", The Matters Group, 2017; https://canna-ventures.com/resources/cannabis-brand-research-summary-2/

## CHAPTER 6

1 "The Book of Bourbon", Distilled Spirits Council; https://www.americanwhiskeytrail.com/american-whiskey-history

2 "Smart Packaging Technologies for Fast Moving Consumer Goods; https://imtk.ui.ac.id/wp-content/uploads/2014/02/Smart-Packaging-Technologies-for-Fast-Moving-Consumer-Goods.pdf

3 "Keywords for Media Studies" By Laurie Ouellette & Jonathan Gray.

4 "What is A Brand", Ignyte Brands; http://www.ignytebrands.com/what-is-a-brand/

5 "What is A Brand", Ignyte Brands; http://www.ignytebrands.com/what-is-a-brand/

6 "The Color Of Cannabis" By David Paleschuck, Dope Magazine, March 2016; https://dopemagazine.com/the-color-of-cannabis/

7 "The Color Of Cannabis" By David Paleschuck, Dope Magazine, March 2016; https://dopemagazine.com/the-color-of-cannabis/

8 "Goethe on the Psychology of Color and Emotion"; https://www.brainpickings.org/2012/08/17/goethe-theory-of-colours/

9 "Psychology Explains How to Choose the Perfect Color for Your Brand", December 2015; https://www.inc.com/help-scout/psychology-explains-how-to-choose-the-perfect-color-for-your-brand.html

10 "The Color Of Cannabis" By David Paleschuck, Dope Magazine, March 2016; https://dopemagazine.com/the-color-of-cannabis/

11 "The Color Of Cannabis" By David Paleschuck, Dope Magazine, March 2016; https://dopemagazine.com/the-color-of-cannabis/

12 "Exciting Red And Competent Blue: The Importance Of Color In Marketing"; Journal of the Academy of Marketing Science, September 2012, Volume 40

13 "The Interactive Effects Of Colors And Products On Perceptions Of Brand Logo Appropriateness"; https://journals.sagepub.com/doi/abs/10.1177/1470593106061263

14 "The Color Of Cannabis" By David Paleschuck, Dope Magazine, March 2016; https://dopemagazine.com/the-color-of-cannabis/

15 "Brand Identity"; http://oer2go.org/mods/en-boundless/www.boundless.com/definition/brand-identity/index.html

16 "Cannabis Brand Study 2017 – Part 1", The Matters Group, 2017; https://canna-ventures.com/product/cannabis-brands-study-v2017/

17 "Cannabis Brand Study 2017 – Part 2", The Matters Group, 2017; https://canna-ventures.com/resources/cannabis-brand-research-summary-2/

18 "The Cannabis Branding Guide", The Matters Group, 2017; https://canna-ventures.com/resources/cannabis-branding-guide/

19 "Cannabis Branding for Men & Women", The Matters Group, 2017; https://canna-ventures.com/resources/men-women-brand-research-white-paper/

20 "Cannabis Brand Study 2017 – Part 1", The Matters Group, 2017; https://canna-ventures.com/product/cannabis-brands-study-v2017/

21 "The Cannabis Branding Guide", The Matters Group, 2017; https://canna-ventures.com/resources/cannabis-branding-guide/

22 "The Cannabis Branding Guide", The Matters Group, 2017; https://canna-ventures.com/resources/cannabis-branding-guide/

## CHAPTER 7

### Introduction

1 "Wellness Center - Marijuana". American University. American University. 2013, December 2013.

2 "Marijuana Vaporizer Provides Same Level Of THC, Fewer Toxins, Study Shows". ScienceDaily, December 2013.; http://www.medicaljane.com/2013/10/23/what-are-dabs-cannabis-concentrates-marijuana-extracts-explained/

3 The Washington Post; "Your Kid Is Way More Likely To Be Poisoned By Crayons Than By Marijuana"; Chris Ingraham, July 28th, 2016

4 Pew Research Center; October 12, 2016; Support for marijuana legalization continues to rise; Abigail Geiger; http://www.pewresearch.org/fact-tank/2016/10/12/support-for-marijuana-legalization-continues-to-rise/

5 Your kid is way more likely to be poisoned by crayons than by marijuana; https://www.washingtonpost.com/news/wonk/wp/2016/07/28/your-kid-is-way-more-likely-to-be-poisoned-by-crayons-than-by-marijuana/

6 What Was Hot in Pot in 2018: Top 10 Cannabis Product Trends, December 21, 2018, BDS Analytics; https://bdsanalytics.com/what-was-hot-in-pot-in-2018-cannabis-product-trends/

7 What Was Hot in Pot in 2018: Top 10 Cannabis Product Trends, December 21, 2018, BDS Analytics; https://bdsanalytics.com/what-was-hot-in-pot-in-2018-cannabis-product-trends/

8 What Was Hot in Pot in 2018: Top 10 Cannabis Product Trends, December 21, 2018, BDS Analytics; https://bdsanalytics.com/what-was-hot-in-pot-in-2018-cannabis-product-trends/

9 Current Marijuana Use by Industry and Occupation — Colorado - CDC; https://www.cdc.gov/mmwr/volumes/67/wr/mm6714a1.htm

### Cannabis Flower

10 Current Marijuana Use by Industry and Occupation — Colorado - CDC; https://www.cdc.gov/mmwr/volumes/67/wr/mm6714a1.htm

11 Current Marijuana Use by Industry and Occupation — Colorado - CDC; https://www.cdc.gov/mmwr/volumes/67/wr/mm6714a1.htm

12 Current Marijuana Use by Industry and Occupation — Colorado - CDC; https://www.cdc.gov/mmwr/volumes/67/wr/mm6714a1.htm

13 Current Marijuana Use by Industry and Occupation — Colorado - CDC; https://www.cdc.gov/mmwr/volumes/67/wr/mm6714a1.htm

### Cannabis Concentrates, Oils And Extracts

14 "What Are Cannabis Oil, Shatter, And Wax Extracts?" by Bailey Rahn, May 5, 2015; https://www.leafly.com/news/author/bailey-rahn

15 What Was Hot in Pot in 2018: Top 10 Cannabis Product Trends, December 21, 2018, BDS Analytics; https://bdsanalytics.com/what-was-hot-in-pot-in-2018-cannabis-product-trends/

16 Intro To Vaping - Firefly Blog - Firefly Vapor; https://www.thefirefly.com/blog/2018/07/12/intro-to-vaping/

17 You May Want to Avoid These Ingredients in Cannabis Oil Vape; https://www.leafly.com/news/health/cannabis-vape-oil-ingredients-to-avoid

18 What Was Hot in Pot in 2018: Top 10 Cannabis Product Trends, December 21, 2018, BDS Analytics; https://bdsanalytics.com/what-was-hot-in-pot-in-2018-cannabis-product-trends/

19 What Are Cannabis Topicals and How Do They Work?; www.cvdvt.org/cannabis-topicals-work/

20 What Are Cannabis Topicals and How Do They Work?; www.cvdvt.org/cannabis-topicals-work/

21 What Is CBD And How Is It Different From Marijuana?; https://qz.com/quartzy/.../cbd-the-next-big-thing-in-marijuana-wont-get-you-high/

## Cannabis Edibles

22 A New American Consumer Culture | United States History; https://courses.lumenlearning.com/atd-hostos.../a-new-american-consumer-culture/

23 Washington State Adopts New Warning Label for Edibles; https://www.leafly.com/news/.../washington-state-adopts-new-warning-label-edibles

24 What Was Hot in Pot in 2018: Top 10 Cannabis Product Trends, December 21, 2018, BDS Analytics; https://bdsanalytics.com/what-was-hot-in-pot-in-2018-cannabis-product-trends/

25 What Was Hot in Pot in 2018: Top 10 Cannabis Product Trends, December 21, 2018, BDS Analytics; https://bdsanalytics.com/what-was-hot-in-pot-in-2018-cannabis-product-trends/

## Cannabis Beverages

26 11-Hydroxy-THC - Increased Potency That Explains the Effect of ...; profofpot.com/11-hydroxy-tetrahydrocannabinol-potency-edibles/

## Cannabis Tinctures And Capsules

27 "Marijuana Tinctures: Your Complete Guide"; https://honestmarijuana.com/marijuana-tinctures/

28 "Cannabis Tinctures 101: What Are They, How to Make Them, and How to Use Them"; https://www.leafly.com/news/cannabis-101/cannabis-tinctures-101-what-are-they-how-to-make-them-and-how-to

29 More about Cannabis Capsules; https://weedmaps.com/learn/dictionary/capsule/

30 What's the deal with cannabis capsules?; https://www.thegrowthop.com/cannabis-business/whats-the-deal-with-cannabis-capsules

31 More about Cannabis Capsules; https://weedmaps.com/learn/dictionary/capsule/

32 Cannabis Capsules: Why They Might Be Right for You; HelloMD; https://www.hellomd.com/health-wellness/599a4c1a6dfe300c0a8bac1e/cannabis-capsules-why-they-might-be-right-for-you

## Innovative Cannabis Products

33 "Cannabis Brand Study 2017 – Part 1", The Matters Group, 2017; https://canna-ventures.com/product/cannabis-brands-study-v2017/

## Conclusion

34 "Cannabis Brand Study 2017 – Part 1", The Matters Group, 2017; https://canna-ventures.com/product/cannabis-brands-study-v2017/

35 "Cannabis Brand Study 2017 – Part 1", The Matters Group, 2017; https://canna-ventures.com/product/cannabis-brands-study-v2017/

36 "Cannabis Brand Study 2017 – Part 2", The Matters Group, 2017; https://canna-ventures.com/resources/cannabis-brand-research-summary-2/

37 "Cannabis Branding for Men & Women", The Matters Group, 2017; https://canna-ventures.com/resources/men-women-brand-research-white-paper/

38 "Cannabis Branding in the Golden State", The Matters Group, 2017; https://canna-ventures.com/resources/california-cannabis-brand-research-white-paper/

39 "The Cannabis Branding Guide", The Matters Group, 2017; https://canna-ventures.com/resources/cannabis-branding-guide/

## CHAPTER 8

1 What's in a Brand Name: the Sounds of Persuasion; https://daily.jstor.org/whats-brand-name-sounds-persuasion/

2 Why Color Matters - Colorcom; https://www.colorcom.com/research/why-color-matters

3 Marketing of the 21st Century Marketing Science Institute Research ...; https://www.utwente.nl/...%20widgets%20bij%20news%20items/.../volume-1-essays-0...

4 Exciting red and competent blue: the importance of color in branding & marketing; www.academia.edu/.../Exciting_red_and_competent_blue_the_importance_of_color_...

5 The Importance Of Color In Brand Strategy, Branding Strategy Insider; https://www.brandingstrategyinsider.com/.../the-importance-of-color-in-brand-strateg...

6 Jennifer Aaker, Stanford Graduate School of Business; https://www.gsb.stanford.edu/faculty-research/faculty/jennifer-lynn-aaker

7 The Importance of Colors in marketing and Branding; https://www.shoppingcartelite.com/.../the-importance-of-colors-in-marketing-and-bra...

8 The Psychology of Colors in Marketing and Branding; https://www.noupe.com/.../the-psychology-of-colors-in-marketing-and-branding-990...

9 Color Psychology: How Colors Influence the Mind | Psychology Today; https://www.psychologytoday.com/.../color-psychology-how-colors-influence-the-mi...

10 The Psychology of Color in Marketing and Branding - Help Scout; https://www.helpscout.com › Blog › Growth

11 The Psychology of Colors in Marketing - Dignitas Digital; https://www.dignitasdigital.com/blog/the-psychology-of-colors-in-marketing-part-2/

12 The Psychology Of Colors And How To Create A Strong Brand; www.socialsongbird.com › digital marketing › How to › latest › x-featured-x

## CHAPTER 9

1 Picture of Americia Poisoning Fact Sheet - CDC; https://www.cdc.gov/pictureofamerica/pdfs/Picture_of_America_Poisoning.pdf

2 Protecting Health - CDC; www.cdc.gov/media/pressrel/ProtectingHealth_ForLife_04.pdf

3 Research reveals scale of child-proof packaging problems; https://www.in-pharmatechnologist.com/.../Research-reveals-scale-of-child-proof-pack...

4 It's Not Easy Being Green: Navigating Pesticides in Cannabis; https://dopemagazine.com/navigating-pesticides-in-cannabis/

5 Pesticide Use on Marijuana - Washington State Department of Agriculture; https://agr.wa.gov/pestfert/pesticides/pesticideuseonmarijuana.aspx

6 Cannabis Business Times; Systemic Pesticides; May 2017; magazine.cannabisbusinesstimes.com/.../may.../systemic-pesticides-are-your-clones-at-...

## CHAPTER 10

1 "The 2016 Washington Cannabis Industry: No Signs of Slowing Down", Headset Report, "January 25, 2017; https://www.headset.io/blog/the-2016-washington-cannabis-industry-no-signs-of-slowing-down

2 "Every Gram Has Its Price: A Look at Pricing Trends in the Cannabis Industry", April 5, 2017; https://www.headset.io/blog/every-gram-has-its-price-a-look-at-pricing-trends-in-the-cannabis-industry

3 "On the Come Up: Concentrates Category Shows Consistent Growth", Headset Report, August 31, 2017; https://www.headset.io/blog/on-the-come-up-concentrates-category-shows-consistent-growth

4 "Location, Location, Location: The Effects of Geographic Location On A Store's Sales", Headset Report, November 29, 2017; https://www.headset.io/blog/location-location-location-the-effects-of-geographic-location-on-a-stores-sales

5 "Loyalty Programs Pay Off: A Look at the Purchasing Habits of Loyalty Program Participants", Headset Report, July 16, 2018; https://www.headset.io/blog/loyalty-programs-pay-off-a-look-at-the-purchasing-habits-of-loyalty-program-participants

6 "Early Market Trends: California 2018", Headset Report, August 20, 2018; https://www.headset.io/blog/early-market-trends-california-2018

7 Cowen's Collected View of Cannabis, February 25th, 2019

8 Cowen's Collected View of Cannabis, February 25th, 2019

9 Worldwide Legal Cannabis Spending; BDS Analytics; https://bdsanalytics.com/new-report-worldwide-legal-cannabis-spending-hits-12-2-bill...

10 Cannabis Industry Expected to Be Worth $50 Billion by 2026; https://www.bloomberg.com/.../cannabis-industry-to-expand-to-50-billion-by-2026-a...

11 Americans with Criminal Records - The Sentencing Project - www.sentencingproject.org

# BRANDING BUD

## SUMMIT & PODCAST

Hosted by David Paleschuck, author of

*"Branding Bud: The Commercialization Of Cannabis"*

Learn about the intricacies of cannabis branding with today's most successful cannabis brand builders. Hear their stories. See their brand assets. Understand their brand strategies.

### FIND OUT MORE AT

 linkedin.com/in/brandingbudsummit  @brandingbudsummit  @brandingbudsummit  @brandingbudsummit